Revelation's Seal Team Six

Revelation's Seal Team Six

Evaluating the Timing of the Rapture

CHRISTOPHER WALLS

RESOURCE *Publications* · Eugene, Oregon

REVELATION'S SEAL TEAM SIX
Evaluating the Timing of the Rapture

Resource Publications
An Imprint of Wipf and Stock Publishers
199 W. 8th Ave., Suite 3
Eugene, OR 97401

www.wipfandstock.com

PAPERBACK ISBN: 978-1-6667-3239-9
HARDCOVER ISBN: 978-1-6667-2605-3
EBOOK ISBN: 978-1-6667-2606-0

11/10/21

CONTENTS

1

Where to Begin

MANY BOOKS HAVE BEEN written attempting to determine the timing of the Rapture. The main positions on the matter include the pre-tribulation, mid-tribulation, post-tribulation, and pre-wrath, views. Typically, a writer will either set out to prove that their particular view is correct or that another is incorrect, or simply to seek to help the reader understand all of the differing positions.

When wading through all of the available discussions, it is easy to get overwhelmed and conclude that identifying the order of end-time events is impossible. However, this does not have to be the case. Instead of seeking to prove or disprove a particular view, a systematic study of the available scriptural evidence should be conducted. Rather than focusing on individual arguments, the emphasis should be on allowing Scripture to speak and seeking to gain from the "whole council of God" (Acts 20:27) on this matter.

What should be avoided as much as humanly possible is coming into a study assuming a particular position in advance. Whether one holds to any of the above positions—pre-tribulation, mid-tribulation, post-tribulation, or pre-wrath—those positions should be set aside, and, to the best of one's ability, all presuppositions should be removed. Simply investigate the Bible, carefully consider what God has preserved in its pages, and come to a reasonable conclusion on this matter without being overly influenced by sources outside of Scripture.

The beauty of this discussion is that whatever position one holds doesn't matter in the grand scheme. Everyone who believes in Jesus Christ as Lord and Savior will spend eternity with him, regardless of their position on this one topic. However, there could potentially be some bruises along the way to eternity if one holds to a position that turns out not to be true. Because I personally come from a pre-tribulation background, I want to be particularly careful with this view and the harm it could cause if it is incorrect. I want to set aside my presuppositions and biases, seeking to let the Bible determine my view of the Rapture rather than trying to force Scripture to agree with me. At the end of this study, if you do not agree with the conclusions drawn here, rest assured that I will still call you a brother or sister in Christ if you profess Jesus as Lord.

The first observation in studying the Rapture is that the word "rapture" is nowhere to be seen in most English translations of the Bible. What, then, is this word, and what does it mean? The word "rapture" comes from Latin, but the word in the New Testament's original Greek is *harpazo*, meaning "to snatch out or away." This word appears in the New Testament thirteen times, though most of those instances do not pertain to the event at the heart of this study. The Bible reader can rest assured that the word "rapture" does appear in Scripture, just in forms such as "catch up," "plucked," "snatched away," etc.

Knowing that this is a biblical concept, the best place to begin, then, would be to ask this foundational question: Will there be a rapturing of the church at all? Conceptually, the idea finds its origins in the promise Jesus gives his disciples in John 14:1–4:

> Let not your hearts be troubled. Believe in God; believe also in me. In my Father's house are many rooms. If it were not so, would I have told you that I go to prepare a place for you? And if I go and prepare a place for you, I will come again and will take you to myself, that where I am you may be also. And you know the way to where I am going.

Jesus tells the disciples that he is about to go to his "Father's house," the place commonly referred to as heaven. He says that he will prepare a place there for them, and that he will return to take them back to that place. This returning of Christ for believers to take them, or 'snatch them away,' to heaven is the event at the heart of this study. How and when will it take place?

One important observation surrounding the return of Christ is the method by which Jesus went to his Father's house in the first place. This is recorded in Acts 1:9–11:

> And when he had said these things, as they were looking on, he was lifted up, and a cloud took him out of their sight. And while they were gazing into heaven as he went, behold, two men stood by them in white robes, and said, "Men of Galilee, why do you stand looking into heaven? This Jesus, who was taken up from you into heaven, will come in the same way as you saw him go into heaven."

The two angels tell the disciples that Jesus will return in the same way that he left: coming in a "cloud." This detail is where the different views on the Rapture agree: Jesus is going to return for believers on a "cloud" and take them up to heaven, to his Father's house. The primary text describing how this will take place is found in 1 Thess 4:16–17:

> For the Lord himself will descend from heaven with a cry of command, with the voice of an archangel, and with the sound of the trumpet of God. And the dead in Christ will rise first. Then we who are alive, who are left, will be caught up together with them in the clouds to meet the Lord in the air, and so we will always be with the Lord.

The above passages do point to a literal Rapture where Jesus comes down from heaven—in the clouds—to take believers up to heaven. 1 Thessalonians provides a number of other significant details surrounding this event: "a cry of command" (1 Thess 4:16), "the voice of the archangel" (1 Thess 4:16), "the sound of the trumpet of God" (1 Thess 4:16), and believers being "caught up together . . . in the clouds to meet the Lord in the air" (1 Thess 4:17). The "caught up" in verse 17 is the *harpazo*, or rapture. The church is raptured into the clouds to meet Jesus in the air. This is the fulfillment of the promise of John 14 and is consistent with the events of Acts

1, and the details found in 1 Thess 4 will help guide the remainder of this study.

Since there is agreement on the *how* of the Rapture, the details listed above should help in identifying passages in Scripture that deal with Jesus coming to rapture his church. Where else in the New Testament is Jesus riding on the clouds? What other occurrences involve angels, trumpets, or other details that match the description of the Rapture?

> Now concerning the coming of our Lord Jesus Christ and our being gathered together to him, we ask you, brothers . . . (2 Thess 2:1)

The coming of Jesus to gather the church sounds as if it could refer to the Rapture, so 2 Thessalonians is a book that needs careful consideration. Another interesting verse is found in the book of Revelation:

> Then I looked, and behold, a white cloud, and seated on the cloud one like a son of man, with a golden crown on his head, and a sharp sickle in his hand. (Rev 14:14)

As will be seen later, "son of man" is a title that Jesus used for himself many times in the Gospels. One would expect to find references to the Rapture in the book of Revelation, and this verse is worth careful consideration as well. It will be necessary to do an in-depth look at several portions of the last book of the Bible regarding this topic. Another passage that may be related to the Rapture is found in Matt 24:

> Then will appear in heaven the sign of the Son of Man, and then all the tribes of the earth will mourn, and they will see the Son of Man coming on the clouds of heaven with power and great glory. And he will send out his angels with a loud trumpet call, and they will gather his elect from the four winds, from one end of heaven to the other. (Matt 24:30–31)

Those verses are strikingly similar to 1 Thess 4:16–17, with Jesus "on the clouds," along with "angels," "a loud trumpet call," and a gathering of "his elect." Matthew 24, then, should also receive careful consideration during this study on the Rapture.

This provides a starting point for a systematic study of the Rapture. In reading the entirety of Matt 24, it is clear that other significant concepts associated with the Rapture will also need careful study, including the abomination of desolation, the great tribulation, and the day of the LORD.

CONCLUSION

There is enough scriptural evidence to conclude that the Rapture, where believers are "caught up" to meet Jesus in the air on the way to heaven, is a literal event. Passages that share similarities with the description of this event as seen in 1 Thess 4 include Matt 24 (and parallel passages in Mark and Luke), 2 Thess 2, and the book of Revelation. These texts will also concern other important concepts. The intent of the remainder of this study will be to work through these concepts and texts with the intention of determining what the Bible says about the Rapture in an orderly manner, seeking to avoid all biases and presuppositions to the best of our ability.

2

Grasping the Necessary Terms

THE FOUR MAIN POSITIONS regarding the Rapture are pre-tribulation, mid-tribulation, post-tribulation, and pre-wrath. It is clear from the names of the first three that understanding the great tribulation will be foundational to this study. When Jesus speaks of a great tribulation in Matt 24, he relates it to the abomination of desolation, another necessary term. In the passage about Jesus "coming on the clouds," Jesus says the following:

> Immediately after the tribulation of those days the sun will be darkened, and the moon will not give its light, and the stars will fall from heaven, and the powers of the heavens will be shaken. (Matt 24:29)

This description of the sun, moon, and stars is similar to Old Testament prophecies about the day of the LORD, providing a third necessary term for studying the Rapture. Therefore, let's begin with the fundamentals of this discussion before diving into the passages that focus on the Rapture, dealing with the following questions in the following order:

What is the day of the LORD?

What is the abomination of desolation?

What is the great tribulation?

1. WHAT IS THE DAY OF THE LORD?

The first main reference to "the day of the LORD" is found in Isa 2:11–12:

> The haughty looks of man shall be brought low, and the lofty pride of men shall be humbled, and the LORD alone will be exalted in that day. For the LORD of hosts has a day against all that is proud and lofty, against all that is lifted up—and it shall be brought low.

During the time of the prophet Isaiah, the nation of Israel had turned away from the LORD, the God of Israel, and allowed themselves to be influenced by the wealth and religions of foreign nations. Israel made treaties, intermarried, and adopted many of the foreign gods and practices of these other nations. Isaiah was written at a time when Israel was not fully committed to God, and God promised that this problem would be resolved in the future. The beginning of this scripture reads: "It shall come to pass in the latter days that the mountain of the house of the LORD shall be established as the highest of the mountains, and shall be lifted up above the hills; and all the nations shall flow to it" (Isa 2:2).

Sometime in the future (from the time Isaiah was written) God will reign over the entire world, with Jerusalem as his capital. He has "a day against all that is proud and lofty" (Isa 2:12), and the purpose behind this future day is expounded upon in later biblical passages:

> For the LORD has a day of vengeance, a year of recompense for the cause of Zion. (Isa 34:8)

> That day is the day of the Lord GOD of hosts, a day of vengeance, to avenge himself on his foes. The sword shall devour and be sated and drink its fill of their blood. For the Lord GOD of hosts holds a sacrifice in the north country by the river Euphrates. (Jer 46:10)

The "day of the LORD" is also prophesied in the books of Ezekiel, Joel, Amos, Obadiah, Zephaniah, Zechariah, and Malachi, making the day of the LORD one of the most significant topics in the prophetic books of the Old Testament. Some passages describe a worldwide judgment, while others focus primarily on the judgment that will befall Israel. It seems that the nation of Israel was under the impression, possibly from favorable interpretations of texts like Isa 34:8 (above), that the day of the LORD would have God judge the rest of the world but bless Israel. God appears to be correcting that faulty view in places like Amos 5:18: "Woe to you who desire the day of the LORD! Why would you have the day of the LORD? It is darkness, and not light."

On the day of the LORD, God is going to humble everyone who does not serve him, whether or not they are natives of Israel. As for what that day will look like, there is Isa 13:9–10:

> Behold, the day of the LORD comes, cruel, with wrath and fierce anger, to make the land a desolation and to destroy its sinners from it. For the stars of the heavens and their constellations will not give their light; the sun will be dark at its rising, and the moon will not shed its light.

Joel uses very similar language:

> The sun shall be turned to darkness, and the moon to blood, before the great and awesome day of the LORD comes. And it shall come to pass that everyone who calls on the name of the LORD shall be saved. For in Mount Zion and in Jerusalem there shall be those who escape, as the LORD has said, and among the survivors shall be those whom the LORD calls. (Joel 2:31–32)

The prophets describe the day of the LORD as a time of judgment against unbelievers at the hands of God. Joel 2:31 describes cosmic signs that will take place "before the great and awesome day," and Joel 2:32 says that "everyone who calls on the name of the LORD shall be saved" from this judgment. Malachi 4:1–6 also describes this coming day. Here, Malachi says it will bring destruction for evildoers, but healing for "you who fear my name" (4:2). In verse 5, Malachi says, "Behold, I will send you Elijah the prophet before the great and awesome day of the LORD comes."

One's relationship with God determines whether the day of the LORD brings destruction or healing, and two distinct signs are given that will occur *before* this day takes place: cosmic signs where sun, moon, and stars will not give their light, and the appearing of Elijah the prophet. Both of these are said to precede the day of the LORD. That will probably be very important to consider toward the end of this study:

> End-time order of operations:
> Cosmic signs → day of the LORD
> Elijah → day of the LORD

There is no indication, at this point, which of these two signs will come before the other, but *both* of them are supposed to happen before God starts judging the world on that "great and awesome day." With a basic understanding of the Old Testament expectation for the day of the LORD, let's move forward to the second important topic.

2. WHAT IS THE ABOMINATION OF DESOLATION?

An abomination in general is simply something that causes disgust or hatred. In the biblical sense, it is an action that is exceptionally wicked in the eyes of God. In the book of Daniel, there are several mentions of something called "the abomination of desolation," a specific event that will relate to the great tribulation.

Because this may be the least familiar of the important topics related to the Rapture for the average Bible reader, here is a synopsis beforehand: the abomination of desolation is an event where an evil ruler called the antichrist sets himself up as God in the third temple in Jerusalem. References to this event are found in the books of Daniel, Matthew (along with Mark and Luke), and 2 Thessalonians. Now let's consider the scriptural references to the abomination of desolation.

The first reference to this abomination of desolation is found in Dan 9. Daniel has prayed over Israel, which has been in exile for nearly seventy years. Then the angel Gabriel delivers a message from God saying that there are seventy "weeks," or, better translated, seventy "sevens" decreed for the nation of Israel. This passage will be studied more closely later, but there is good reason for understanding this as seventy groups of seven-year periods decreed for Israel.

The first sixty-nine groups of seven-year periods are consecutive, leading up to Jesus Christ:

> Know and understand this: From the time the word goes out to restore and rebuild Jerusalem until the Anointed One, the ruler, comes, there will be seven 'sevens,' and sixty-two 'sevens.' It will be rebuilt with streets and a trench, but in times of trouble. (Dan 9:25 NIV)

God's message to Daniel is that the Messiah will come at a specific time, with 483 years—or sixty-nine groups of seven years—between "the time the word goes out to restore and build Jerusalem" and the appearing of "the Anointed One."

Daniel 9:27 discusses the final seven-year period, but verse 26 indicates that there is an unspecified delay between the final seven and the sixty-nine sevens that came before, based on a number of important details:

> After the sixty-two "sevens," the Anointed One will be put to death and will have nothing. The people of the ruler who will come will destroy the city and the sanctuary. The end will come like a flood: War will continue until the end, and desolations have been decreed. (Dan 9:26 NIV)

Jesus is going to arrive at a specific time, and he is going to die. Historically, this happens around 30 or 33 AD, but the rest of the events of this verse happen much later. In fulfillment of the first part of the verse ("the people of the ruler who will come will destroy the city and the sanctuary"), the temple in Jerusalem was destroyed in 70 AD, around forty years after the death of Christ. Later in the verse, there is also something called "the end," with war and desolations that occur before it. Daniel is not told how long this delay between the first set of "sevens" and the final seven-year period will be, only that between Christ dying and this final period there are several signs: the destruction of the temple and city, war, and desolations.

Then there is Dan 9:27:

> And he shall make a strong covenant with many for one week, and for half of the week he shall put an end to

sacrifice and offering. And on the wing of abominations
shall come one who makes desolate, until the decreed
end is poured out on the desolator.

Where the ESV translates part of the verse as "for half of the
week," most other translations read "in the middle of the week" or
"in the middle of the 'seven.'" Daniel is told about the final seven-
year period: "he"—presumably the "ruler who will come" from verse
26—will make a seven-year covenant, or contract, with "many." Who
exactly is "he," and with whom is he making this covenant? While
these details aren't abundantly clear in the text, at the halfway point
of the seven-year period, this ruler puts "an end to sacrifice and offering." Somewhere called "the wing of abominations" there will be
a person called "one who makes desolate." A few chapters later, these
terms are put together to make "the abomination of desolation," but
first let's make some observations about this verse.

Since this whole prophecy revolves around Israel and sacrifices can only be made in the temple at Jerusalem, there are a number of things that can reasonably be determined. In Dan 9:26, the
temple was destroyed, but now in verse 27 the temple must have
been rebuilt so that sacrifices can take place again. These sacrifices
require a third temple that, at the time of this writing, has not yet
been built. It appears that the final seven-year period discussed in
Dan 9 is still a future event.

In Dan 11, the author receives a very detailed prophetic account of events surrounding military powers in the Middle East—
namely, Persia, Greece, and Rome. Something significant for this
study is recorded in Dan 11:31, which says, "Forces from him shall
appear and profane the temple and fortress, and shall take away the
regular burnt offering. And they shall set up the abomination that
makes desolate."

These activities match what is recorded in 1 Macc 1:45–46.
Most Protestant Christians may not be familiar with 1–2 Maccabees,
since they are not found in the Bibles they typically reference. These
are some of the Deuterocanonical, or Apocryphal, books. While
they may not be considered inspired Scripture, they may have value
as historical writings that relate to the events described in Dan 11.

In 1 Macc 1:45–46, Antiochus IV Epiphanes orders pigs to be sacrificed at the temple, matching the "abomination that makes desolate" from Dan 11:31. While the events of the Maccabees take place in the second century BC, Jesus referred to a future "abomination of desolation" in Matt 24:15, indicating that this historical event was something of a preview of what would take place in the future. This future event is what is described in Dan 9:27. Even later, in Dan 11:35, it indicates that there are still events far in the future that will be played out in "the time of the end."

This idea of end times is repeated in Dan 12:

> Go your way, Daniel, for the words are shut up and sealed until the time of the end. Many shall purify themselves and make themselves white and be refined, but the wicked shall act wickedly. And none of the wicked shall understand, but those who are wise shall understand. And from the time that the regular burnt offering is taken away and the abomination that makes desolate is set up, there shall be 1,290 days. (Dan 12:9–11)

The time mentioned in the verse—1,290 days—is approximately three and a half years, lining up well with Dan 9:27, which says that the final seven-year period will be broken in half. These words in Dan 12 seem to be referring to the same event described in Dan 9.

An "abomination of desolation" is mentioned three times in the book: Dan 9:27, 11:31, and 12:11. In the New Testament, Jesus picks this topic up in Matt 24 when his disciples ask him about the "end of the age":

> So when you see the abomination of desolation spoken of by the prophet Daniel, standing in the holy place (let the reader understand), then let those who are in Judea flee to the mountains. (Matt 24:15–16)

While Antiochus IV Epiphanes already did the abominable thing mentioned in Dan 11:31—sacrificing pigs to false gods on God's altar—over a hundred years earlier, Jesus says another abominable event will take place in the temple in the future. Jesus warns them that when they see this abominable act take place, they need to flee if they are living around Jerusalem. Paul appears to write about the same event in 2 Thess 2 in response to some Christians thinking that they had already missed the second coming of Christ.

> Let no one deceive you in any way. For that day will not come, unless the rebellion comes first, and the man of lawlessness is revealed, the son of destruction, who opposes and exalts himself against every so-called god or object of worship, so that he takes his seat in the temple of God, proclaiming himself to be God. (2 Thess 2:3–4)

When considering Daniel, Matthew, and 2 Thessalonians collectively, it appears that the abomination of desolation is the act of this future evil ruler setting himself up to be God in the third temple in Jerusalem. This event will take place halfway through an agreement that this ruler will make, either with Israel, the enemies of Israel, or both. Better understanding the details surrounding this event should help in the effort to determine how all of the end-time events work together, and specifically where in the time line of these events the Rapture comes into play.

Another name requires discussion regarding the abomination of desolation: the antichrist. This is a title that is only found in 1–2 John, where the name is used four times. The first two occurrences seem to link this antichrist with the ruler that causes the abomination of desolation.

> Children, it is the last hour, and as you have heard that antichrist is coming, so now many antichrists have come. Therefore we know that it is the last hour. (1 John 2:18)

> Who is the liar but he who denies that Jesus is the Christ? This is the antichrist, he who denies the Father and the Son. (1 John 2:22)

"Antichrist" literally means "against Christ" or "adversary of Christ." According to 1 John 2:18, believers were aware that this enemy of Christ was coming in relation to "the last hour." Just a few verses later, John seems to say that anyone who denies that Jesus is the Christ is, in some way, associated with the antichrist. "Christ" and "Messiah" are both terms that refer to the future king of the world, and the Bible firmly establishes that this title belongs to Jesus. Some adversary is going to deny that Jesus is the Christ, and this adversary is present at "the last hour."

The "evil ruler" mentioned in Daniel and the "man of lawlessness" mentioned in 2 Thessalonians both fit this description of the adversary of Christ. These are, most likely, all the same person. The antichrist will make the seven-year deal where Israel is able to make sacrifices in the third temple in Jerusalem. This antichrist will stop those sacrifices three and a half years into that deal, deny that Jesus is the Christ, and proclaim himself to be God in that third temple. This event is called the abomination of desolation.

3. WHAT IS THE GREAT TRIBULATION?

The end of Dan 11 points toward future events beyond the time of the first coming of Christ, as indicated by Dan 9:26–27. Daniel 12:1 continues talking about this future time period:

> At that time shall arise Michael, the great prince who has charge of your people. And there shall be a time of trouble, such as never has been since there was a nation till that time. But at that time your people shall be delivered, everyone whose name shall be found written in the book. (Dan 12:1)

A future time of trouble will take place that is worse than anything Israel had experienced up to the life of Daniel, which is significant, since Daniel was living through a seventy-year exile. In Matt 24, after telling the disciples to be on the lookout for the abomination of desolation spoken of in Daniel, Jesus says, "For then there will be great tribulation, such as has not been from the beginning of the world until now, no, and never will be" (Matt 24:21). This great tribulation will be worse than the four hundred years of slavery in Egypt (recorded in Exodus), worse than the seventy years of exile in Babylon that Daniel experienced, worse than anything Antiochus or Rome did, and even worse than the horrors the Jewish people experienced during the Holocaust. Nothing in all of human history will be as terrible as what is coming in what Jesus describes as the "great tribulation."

Finally, this same event is mentioned in Rev 7:14:

> These are the ones coming out of the great tribulation. They have washed their robes and made them white in the blood of the Lamb.

This raises an important point: all of the terms currently under review will be described in the book of Revelation. However, it would be wise to understand all of these terms and what the Bible says about them elsewhere before seeking to add to our understanding about them from the final book of the Bible.

CONCLUSION

The Rapture was discussed in the previous chapter. Now, the day of the LORD, the abomination of desolation, and the great tribulation have also been investigated. The rest of this study will take into consideration the related passages in Matthew, 1–2 Thessalonians, and Revelation in an effort to place these four biblical concepts in some kind of chronological order.

3

Jesus in Matthew 24

IN DAN 9, THERE is a final seven-year period in God's plan for the nation of Israel. Halfway through that period, an evil ruler, the antichrist, will end sacrifices in the third temple and will set up the abomination of desolation. Jesus speaks on this very issue in Matt 24, with parallel passages found in Mark 13 and Luke 21. Let's consider Matt 24:1–37. You are welcome to prayerfully read through the passage in its entirety before continuing in this book so that you have a working knowledge of the whole text.

In verses 1–3, Jesus is walking with his disciples away from the temple when he tells them something that they likely found unbelievable at the time: "You see all these, do you not [as they look at the Second Temple in Jerusalem]? Truly, I say to you, there will not be left here one stone upon another" (Matt 24:2). How could such a beautiful structure be so utterly destroyed? Once they were outside of the city, at the Mount of Olives, the disciples ask Jesus three questions: first, when the destruction of the temple will happen; second, what will be the sign of Jesus' coming; third, what will be the sign of the end of the age. Technically, the disciples likely lumped the second and third questions together, seeing Jesus' second coming and the end of the age as synonymous events. Jesus seems largely to ignore the first question about the destruction of the temple, instead focusing on the latter two.

What Jesus said about the destruction of the temple was already foretold in Dan 9.

> After the sixty-two "sevens," the Anointed One will be put to death and will have nothing. The people of the ruler who will come will destroy the city and the sanctuary. The end will come like a flood: war will continue until the end, and desolations have been decreed. (Dan 9:26 NIV)

After Jesus died on the cross, there would be people associated with the future evil ruler. They would destroy both the city and the sanctuary [temple]. Jesus prophesied about this event, focusing specifically on the temple and saying that "there will not be left here one stone upon another" (Matt 24:2). History reveals that this event took place in 70 AD, with General Titus of Rome sacking the city. According to Flavius Josephus, a Jewish historian working for Rome, it was not Titus's intention to have the temple destroyed, but it ultimately caught fire. Either way, the words of Jesus were true, as the temple was destroyed around forty years after his declaration.

The words in Dan 9:26–27 indicate that terrible things will happen between the destruction of the temple and the events of the final seven-year period. Jesus' answer to the disciples about the signs of his coming and the end of the age in Matt 24 is very much related to the brief description in Dan 9.

Beginning in Matt 24:4, Jesus tells the disciples not to be deceived and lists the signs related to the return of Christ. The list begins with many false messiahs proclaiming themselves to be Christ, then includes wars, famines, earthquakes, and such. "War is a sign of Jesus' return!" is a common modern phrase. Read Matt 24:6 carefully:

> And you will hear of wars and rumors of wars. See that you are not alarmed, for this must take place, but the end is not yet.

Notice how Jesus says that wars and rumors of wars are *not* the sign of his coming. In verse 3, the disciples asked for a definitive sign of Jesus' second coming, and Jesus will provide that sign.

However, there are many other signs that Jesus gives that do not definitively mark his return. Everything that Jesus says in verses 5–14 will absolutely take place leading up to the end of the age. There will be false messiahs, false prophets, wars, natural disasters, persecutions, and many "believers" falling away, as well as the gospel going out to the whole world. But most, if not all, of those signs can be seen today, and have been seen throughout the last two thousand years. They are signs, but they are not *the* sign. Jesus specifically answers the disciples' question in verse 15.

> So when you see standing in the holy place "the abomination that causes desolation," spoken of through the prophet Daniel—let the reader understand—then let those who are in Judea flee to the mountains. (Matt 24:15–16)

The disciples wanted to know the sign of Jesus' return. According to Jesus, the sign they need to look for is when the antichrist sets up the abomination that causes desolation from Dan 9. During that final seven-year period for Israel, the Jews will be able to offer sacrifices in the new temple for the first three and a half years. After those three and a half years, the antichrist will stop those sacrifices and initiate the abomination of desolation.

Paul wrote of this event in 2 Thessalonians. The church in Thessalonica had been told they had already missed Jesus' second coming, and they were very concerned. Paul's response was:

> Concerning the coming of our Lord Jesus Christ and our being gathered to him, we ask you, brothers and sisters, not to become easily unsettled or alarmed by the teaching allegedly from us—whether by a prophecy or by word of mouth or by letter—asserting that the day of the Lord has already come. Don't let anyone deceive you in any way, for that day will not come until the rebellion occurs and the man of lawlessness is revealed, the man doomed to destruction. He will oppose and will exalt himself over everything that is called God or is worshiped, so that he sets himself up in God's temple, proclaiming himself to be God. (2 Thess 2:1–4 NIV)

Paul mentions a man, called the man of lawlessness, who is doomed to destruction. Daniel 9:27 ended with "the decreed end [that] is poured out on the desolator." In Thessalonians, this "man of lawlessness . . . sets himself up in God's temple, proclaiming himself to be God" (2 Thess 2:3–4). Jesus says that the abomination of desolation spoken of in Daniel would stand "in the holy place" (Matt 24:15). All of these passages work together to describe the same event: the antichrist will stop the sacrifices that take place in the third temple and will set himself up to be God in the holy place, which is the main room in the temple. Jesus told his disciples that when they see *that* sign—the antichrist setting up the abomination of desolation—they need to literally "flee to the mountains" (Matt 24:16). In Matt 24:17–20, he tells them that they need to run quickly, and that it will be terrible for pregnant women and nursing mothers. Why is this so?

> For then there will be great tribulation, such as has not been from the beginning of the world until now, no, and never will be. (Matt 24:21)

The great tribulation is coined from this passage, and is also mentioned in Dan 12:1 and Rev 7:14. Jesus says this will be the single greatest period of distress in the world's history. No battle, war, or tragedy will compare to this event. This great tribulation is so devastating that Jesus says a time limit has been placed on it.

> And if those days had not been cut short, no human being would be saved. But for the sake of the elect those days will be cut short. (Matt 24:22)

This verse raises a few questions. What does "those days will be shortened" mean? Was there a previously set length of time for the great tribulation to occur, but now Jesus is shortening that time? One interpretation of "those days will be shortened" is that the great tribulation will be a relatively short period of time. If the abomination of desolation happens halfway through the final seven-year period for Israel and the great tribulation happens after the abomination of desolation, then the great tribulation will only last for three and a half years. That's pretty short in the grand scheme of things. This is a fair interpretation of "those days will be shortened."

Another consideration about Matt 24:22 involves the identity of "the elect." It was "for the sake of the elect" that the tribulation gets a time limit. From a Jewish perspective, "the elect" would represent Israel. However, the term "elect" throughout the New Testament refers specifically to believers in Christ. Further context is needed to determine who "the elect" are in this passage.

> At that time if anyone says to you, "Look, here is the Messiah!" or, "There he is!" do not believe it. For false messiahs and false prophets will appear and perform great signs and wonders to deceive, if possible, even the elect. See, I have told you ahead of time. (Matt 24:23–25 NIV)

While false messiahs and false prophets have existed throughout the history of Christianity, Jesus is specifically referring to counterfeits during the great tribulation, and more details about these specific frauds will be revealed in the book of Revelation. Their signs and wonders will be so convincing that, if it were possible, they would fool even the elect. Israel may be God's chosen people, but time and time again they have fallen away to serve false gods, even some of their own making, like the golden calf in Exod 32. The antichrist will fool the whole world, and no doubt will fool many Israelites as well. But the ones who will see through the deception will be the ones who hold to the words of Jesus. Jesus says, "See, I have told you ahead of time" (Matt 24:25). This forewarning from Jesus is why it will be impossible to deceive the elect. This points to the elect being Christians rather than the nation of Israel as a whole. Christians will not be fooled, because they will hold to the words of Jesus, who told them in advance about the deceptions of the antichrist.

As seen in Matt 24:22, this means that the great tribulation will be "cut short" on account of Christians, which places at least some Christians on earth during the great tribulation. False messiahs and false prophets will fool many people, but whatever Christians are present during this time will know the words of Jesus and not be fooled. Jesus prepares these Christians to identify imposters in this way:

So if anyone tells you, "There he is, out in the wilderness," do not go out; or, "Here he is, in the inner rooms," do not believe it. For as lightning that comes from the east is visible even in the west, so will be the coming of the Son of Man. Wherever there is a carcass, there the vultures will gather. (Matt 24:26–28 NIV)

Jesus' coming will be as obvious as lightning in the sky. He won't be reincarnated, and he won't be hiding in a desert, forest, cave, or monastery. He will descend from heaven in much the same way that he ascended to heaven in Acts 1.

After he said this, he was taken up before their very eyes, and a cloud hid him from their sight. They were looking intently up into the sky as he was going, when suddenly two men dressed in white stood beside them. "Men of Galilee," they said, "why do you stand here looking into the sky? This same Jesus, who has been taken from you into heaven, will come back in the same way you have seen him go into heaven. (Acts 1:9–11 NIV)

Jesus rose up to heaven, and he will come back down from heaven. His appearing will be obvious, just like lightning is clearly visible in the sky, or, as Jesus said in Matt 24:28, like a vulture flying around clearly means there is a carcass nearby. What will this obvious event look like?

Immediately after the tribulation of those days the sun will be darkened, and the moon will not give its light, and the stars will fall from heaven, and the powers of the heavens will be shaken. Then will appear in heaven the sign of the Son of Man, and then all the tribes of the earth will mourn, and they will see the Son of Man coming on the clouds of heaven with power and great glory. (Matt 24:29–30)

The sun turning dark, the moon not giving light, and the stars falling from the sky are all language that has appeared throughout the Old Testament regarding the day of the LORD and that marks God's judgment of the earth. These are cosmic events, with the "heavenly bodies" being shaken. Jesus said his coming would be obvious. What happens after the world sees these cosmic events? "Then will appear the sign of the Son of Man in heaven." The Son of Man is a title Jesus has used multiple times in Matthew to identify himself, and this whole chapter has been about his return. According to Matt 24:30, Jesus will appear on the clouds of heaven in a powerful display that causes all of the people of the earth to mourn.

> And he will send his angels with a loud trumpet call, and they will gather his elect from the four winds, from one end of the heavens to the other. (Matt 24:31)

Knowing that "the elect" are Christians, this appears to be about the Rapture. In fact, it is quite similar to 1 Thess 4:16–17 (NIV), the most famous Rapture passage:

> For the Lord himself will come down from heaven, with a loud command, with the voice of the archangel and with the trumpet call of God, and the dead in Christ will rise first. After that, we who are still alive and are left will be caught up together with them in the clouds to meet the Lord in the air. And so we will be with the Lord forever.

The similarities between these two passages are striking, and it would be difficult to believe that these are not describing the same event. "And he will send his angels" parallels "the voice of the archangel." "With a loud trumpet call" matches "the trumpet call of God." In Matt 24, Jesus is "on the clouds of heaven," and in 1 Thess 4, Christians are "caught up together . . . in the clouds to meet the Lord in the air." Everything lines up so precisely that it seems clear that if Paul is describing the Rapture in 1 Thessalonians, then Jesus is describing the Rapture of the church in Matt 24:31.

Some might argue that the language of Matt 24:31, specifically "from one end of the heavens to the other," might indicate that Jesus is gathering his elect who have already been in heaven. Both Mark and Luke describe parallel passages. While Luke does not have a verse that parallels Matt 24:31, Mark does:

> And then he will send out the angels and gather his elect from the four winds, from the ends of the earth to the ends of heaven. (Mark 13:27)

This verse makes it clear that this great gathering also has Christians living on earth in view. Let's take a moment to acknowledge what this sounds like. Jesus' words appear to place the Rapture of the church after the abomination of desolation and at least part of the way through the great tribulation. Let's consider the rest of the passage before trying to straighten out our thoughts.

KNOW THE SIGNS

> Now learn this lesson from the fig tree: As soon as its twigs get tender and its leaves come out, you know that summer is near. Even so, when you see all these things, you know that it is near, right at the door. (Matt 24:32–33 NIV)

The illustration Jesus gives is simple to understand. By looking at a fig tree and understanding the signs, you can tell that summer is near. The twigs will get tender and the leaves will come out. Likewise, seeing the appropriate signs will reveal that Jesus is near. What are the definitive signs? They aren't wars, famines, false prophets, or "Christians" turning away from the faith. Paul expressed in 2 Thessalonians that the antichrist will be revealed before Jesus comes. The antichrist will set himself up as God in the third temple in Jerusalem halfway through the final seven-year period for Israel, and that will mark the beginning of the great tribulation. This antichrist is the telltale sign that Jesus is coming soon. What follows his abominable act in the temple are three and a half years of terrible tribulation. However, at some point during that time, cosmic events will take place (sun, moon, stars) and Jesus will appear in the sky, gathering all Christians together to be with him in the air.

What follows after the Rapture of the church is the day of the LORD, which will bring judgment for the inhabitants of the world.

THIS GENERATION

> Truly I tell you, this generation will certainly not pass away until all these things have happened. Heaven and

earth will pass away, but my words will never pass away. (Matt 24:34–35 NIV)

Who is "this generation"? While the current audience Jesus is speaking to would seem the obvious answer, Dan 9 causes a problem for this interpretation. In Dan 9:26, the temple is destroyed, but in the very next verse, the abomination is set up inside the temple, necessitating a third temple. A third temple, even to the date of this publication, has not yet been constructed. "This generation" must be something other than those to whom Jesus was speaking.

Take a moment to look at the pronouns Jesus used throughout Matt 24:

- Verse 6: "You will hear of wars and rumors of wars."

- Verse 9: "Then you will be handed over to be persecuted and put to death."

Now, if "you" was specifically referring to the disciples, then there should be no more references to "you," because they were killed in verse 9. However, this is not the case.

- Verse 15: "So when you see standing in the holy place 'the abomination that causes desolation' . . ."

Clearly, "you" is not specifically referring to the disciples with whom Jesus was speaking. "You" will see wars, be persecuted and put to death, and will see the abomination set up in the third temple. "You" seems to be referring to Christians in general, or a specific group of Christians. Are Christians going to experience the great tribulation? Verse 21 describes it, then verse 22 says it is cut short for the sake of "the elect," or Christians.

- Verse 23: "At that time [of the great tribulation] if anyone says to you, 'Look, here is the Christ!' or, 'There he is!' do not believe it."

Now, whatever group "you" represents has seen the abomination of desolation and the great tribulation. Could the Rapture take place before these two events if Jesus tells his disciples that "you" will experience these things? If all of these things happened during the lifetimes of the disciples, Jesus seems to indicate that they would be among those experiencing the great tribulation.

In verse 30, there is a different pronoun, as Jesus is speaking of a different group of people.

- Verse 30: "Then will appear the sign of the Son of Man in heaven. And then all the peoples of the earth will mourn when they see the Son of Man coming on the clouds of heaven, with power and great glory."

Christians have been the "you" throughout this chapter. When Jesus appears in the sky to take "you" home, "they" will mourn. "They" might even see "you" leave, which will be a glorious thing for one pronoun, but a terrible thing for the other.

- Verse 33: "Even so, when you see all these things, you know that it is near, right at the door."

So, "you" is the group of Christians that will see all these things. They will see the abomination of desolation, the great tribulation, and the appearance of Christ in the sky for the Rapture, and it appears these three things will happen in that order. Now the meaning of Jesus' words in verse 34 becomes clear: "this generation" is not specifically the disciples. "This generation" is the group of Christians who see the abomination and go through the tribulation. What Jesus is saying is simply a repeat of the main idea of verse 22: these events will not cover an exceptionally long period of time. There have been nearly two thousand years between the first sixty-nine "sevens" from Daniel and the last "seven," but when that last time period begins, it will not linger. You (Christians) have been waiting for generations for the Day of the LORD. When the true sign begins, "you know that it is near, right at the door" (Matt 24:33).

Just because you know that it is near doesn't mean you know exactly when that day will come:

> But concerning that day and hour no one knows, not even the angels of heaven, nor the Son, but the Father only. For as were the days of Noah, so will be the coming of the Son of Man. (Matt 24:36–37)

The rest of the passage is Jesus speaking about the Rapture, where one person will be taken up and another person left. This rapturing is directly associated with "the coming of the Son of Man." Verse 30 says that "all the people of the earth will mourn, and they will see the Son of Man coming"

In Matt 24, Jesus appears to offer the end-time events in the following order: the abomination of desolation, the great tribulation, and then the Rapture/day of the LORD.

THOSE DAYS CUT SHORT

In Dan 9, there is a seven-year period for the Israelites in which the evil ruler stops sacrifices three and a half years in. Looking back at Dan 7, Daniel receives a dream about four kingdoms that will rise to power over the earth. Daniel is told about what will happen with the fourth kingdom.

> The ten horns are ten kings who will come from this kingdom. After them another king will arise, different from the earlier ones; he will subdue three kings. He will speak against the Most High and oppress his holy people and try to change the set times and the laws. The holy people will be delivered into his hands for a time, times and half a time. (Dan 7:24–25 NIV)

From the passage in Dan 9, as well as the statement here about changing "the set times and the laws," it is clear that "his holy people" refers to the nation of Israel in Daniel 7:24–25. This "different" king, the antichrist, will oppress the "holy people" for three and a half years (a time, times, and half a time). That would appear to take place after the three and a half years of relative peace, which results in a total of seven years. Perhaps it is best to see the great tribulation as happening only the last half of the seven years, rather than that full time period. According to Daniel, the Israelites must go through the full three and a half years of the great tribulation. What about "the elect" from Matt 24? What if when Jesus said "for the sake of the elect those days will be shortened" this means that the Christians, while going through the great tribulation, do not experience the full three and a half years? Perhaps the Christians are taken out before those years of tribulation decreed for Israel are completed. When Matt 24:29 says, "immediately after the distress of those days," it may be referring to the portion of the tribulation that the Christians must experience before they are gathered together by the angels. If this is the case, then both Dan 9 and Matt 24 are correct in their timing statements: Israel will endure three and a half years of the tribulation, while Christians will go through an amount of time less than that because their time will be cut short.

CONCLUSION

In Matt 24, Jesus gives this order for the end-time events: abomination of desolation, great tribulation, Rapture/day of the LORD. With that general outline in mind, the Rapture of the elect could take place part of the way through the great tribulation.

Jesus says the abomination of desolation will be revealed first, and that this event will be the definitive sign that Jesus is coming very soon. The abomination marks the beginning of the great tribulation. Either at the end of the tribulation or somewhere in the midst of it, possibly cutting those days short for believers, Jesus will descend from heaven and the Rapture will take place—using language nearly identical to the clear Rapture passage of 1 Thess 4:16–17. Jesus' coming is immediately preceded by the cosmic signs associated with the day of the LORD, meaning that Matt 24 talks about all four of the key terms: abomination of desolation, great tribulation, Rapture, and day of the LORD.

4

1–2 Thessalonians

THERE ARE TWO VERSES in 1 Thessalonians that are frequently used in discussions surrounding the Rapture of the church:

> And to wait for his Son from heaven, whom he raised from the dead, Jesus who delivers us from the wrath to come. (1 Thess 1:10)

> For God has not destined us for wrath, but to obtain salvation through our Lord Jesus Christ. (1 Thess 5:9)

On several different occasions, these verses have been used to support the pre-tribulation Rapture position. Because "God has not destined us for wrath," we must, therefore, not go through the great tribulation. But, when Paul says "wrath to come," is he referencing the great tribulation? What else does Paul say in this letter and in his follow-up letter?

Something seen in both of Paul's letters to the Thessalonians is that at the time of Paul's writing, this church is experiencing persecution. They are going through a tribulation when they receive these encouraging letters:

> For you, brothers, became imitators of the churches of God in Christ Jesus that are in Judea. For you suffered the same things from your own countrymen as they did from the Jews. (1 Thess 2:14)

> This is evidence of the righteous judgment of God, that
> you may be considered worthy of the kingdom of God,
> for which you are also suffering. (2 Thess 1:5)

The Thessalonians are experiencing tribulation, but they are
not experiencing the great tribulation, which is still a future event.
There is also a future "wrath" that, according to Paul, Christians
are not destined to experience. Is that wrath the great tribulation?
This should not immediately be assumed unless clearly stated in
Scripture.

So, what does Paul say, if anything, about the four key terms
studied previously (Day of the LORD, abomination of desolation,
great tribulation, and Rapture)? In his first letter, there are multiple
references to the second coming of Christ:

> For what is our hope or joy or crown of boasting before
> our Lord Jesus at his coming? Is it not you? For you are
> our glory and joy. (1 Thess 2:19–20)

> So that he may establish your hearts blameless in holi-
> ness before our God and Father, at the coming of our
> Lord Jesus with all his saints. (1 Thess 3:13)

By mentioning Christ's coming, Paul has certainly taught the
Thessalonians *something* about Christ's return to earth. The faith
of the Thessalonians is something Paul can boast about at Christ's
coming. When Christ comes, it seems that he will be coming "with
all his saints." In the next chapter, Paul has a more in-depth passage
that may explain the phrase "with all his saints."

> But we do not want you to be uninformed, brothers,
> about those who are asleep, that you may not grieve as
> others do who have no hope. For since we believe that
> Jesus died and rose again, even so, through Jesus, God
> will bring with him those who have fallen asleep. For this
> we declare to you by a word from the Lord, that we who
> are alive, who are left until the coming of the Lord, will
> not precede those who have fallen asleep. For the Lord
> himself will descend from heaven with a cry of com-
> mand, with the voice of an archangel, and with the sound
> of the trumpet of God. And the dead in Christ will rise

first. Then we who are alive, who are left, will be caught up together with them in the clouds to meet the Lord in the air, and so we will always be with the Lord. (1 Thess 4:13–17)

There may have been some confusion for the Thessalonians regarding believers in Christ who had died before Jesus returned. At the heart of Paul's words is the encouragement that those who die in Christ before his return have not missed out on his second coming. Just as Jesus rose from the dead, those believers will rise from the dead as well, so that all believers may spend eternity with him. According to verse 15, the dead in Christ will actually see Jesus first. An interesting question arises from this text: Do the dead in Christ rise at his second coming, or are they already with him when he comes down from heaven? According to 1 Thess 4:16, "the dead in Christ will rise first," but in 1 Thess 3:13, it says Jesus will come "with all his saints." It is not the purpose of our study to reach a conclusion regarding the order of events for deceased believers, but the topic is certainly interesting.

What is important for our study is that Paul is referring to the Rapture, where living believers are "caught up" to meet Christ in the air, and Paul gives significant details that should be remembered moving forward: Jesus will "descend from heaven" and there will be "a cry of command, with the voice of an archangel, and with the sound of the trumpet of God" (1 Thess 4:16). Then those who are alive "will be caught up together with them in the clouds to meet the Lord in the air" (1 Thess 4:17). The close of 1 Thess 4 focuses on the Rapture. The Beginning of 1 Thess 5 focuses on the day of the Lord.

> Now concerning the times and the seasons, brothers, you have no need to have anything written to you. For you yourselves are fully aware that the day of the Lord will come like a thief in the night. While people are saying, "There is peace and security," then sudden destruction will come upon them as labor pains come upon a pregnant woman, and they will not escape. (1 Thess 5:1–3)

The order in which Paul writes of these concepts may be important. He wrote about the Rapture in chapter 4 and about the day of the Lord immediately after, in chapter 5. Like Jesus in Matt 24, Paul indicates that people will not know exactly when the day of the Lord is supposed to happen. That doesn't mean that there are no signs indicating it is coming, only that the exact day is not known. The very next verse seems to counter the idea that believers will be unaware that the Rapture/day of the Lord is about to take place:

> But you are not in darkness, brothers, for that day to surprise you like a thief. (1 Thess 5:4)

Paul seems to be making a distinction between believers and unbelievers regarding their awareness of the coming of Christ. Unbelievers will be caught completely off guard, while believers will be keenly aware because they know the signs. What day is Paul referencing? In this letter, Paul has mentioned both the Rapture and the day of the Lord. Is Paul connecting these two concepts in the same way Jesus did in Matt 24?

> But since we belong to the day, let us be sober, having put on the breastplate of faith and love, and for a helmet the hope of salvation. For God has not destined us for wrath, but to obtain salvation through our Lord Jesus Christ. (1 Thess 5:8–9)

Christ's coming again involves both the Rapture and the day of the Lord. Believers are on the lookout for his coming because they know what to look for, being awake and ready rather than asleep and surprised. His coming has believers being raptured, but something altogether different for unbelievers.

When studying the day of the Lord in the Old Testament, Mal 4:1–2 reveals that this event brings destruction for evildoers but healing for the righteous. This would be consistent with Matt 24 and 1 Thess 4–5, where the Rapture and the day of the Lord are connected. When Jesus comes, he will bring the Rapture for believers, but he will bring judgment for unbelievers.

Second Thessalonians 1:5 reveals that the church in Thessalonica is being persecuted. Paul follows that up by saying that God will repay those persecutors for what they've done to the church.

> And to grant relief to you who are afflicted as well as to us, when the Lord Jesus is revealed from heaven with his mighty angels in flaming fire, inflicting vengeance on those who do not know God and on those who do not obey the gospel of our Lord Jesus. They will suffer the punishment of eternal destruction, away from the presence of the Lord and from the glory of his might, when he comes on that day to be glorified in his saints, and to be marveled at among all who have believed, because our testimony to you was believed. (2 Thess 1:7–10)

Paul says that Jesus is coming from heaven and that angels are involved. This is similar to what he wrote in 1 Thess 4:16 about the Rapture. Now, with similar details, Jesus is judging unbelievers, a concept directly connected to the day of the LORD. This seems to agree with what Jesus said in Matt 24, where he connects these two key terms together as well. Jesus' coming from heaven marks both the Rapture and the day of the LORD. Paul has discussed the Rapture and the day of the LORD in his first letter; now it is time for him to share about the abomination of desolation in his second letter.

> Now concerning the coming of our Lord Jesus Christ and our being gathered together to him, we ask you, brothers, not to be quickly shaken in mind or alarmed, either by a spirit or a spoken word, or a letter seeming to be from us, to the effect that the day of the Lord has come. Let no one deceive you in any way. For that day will not come, unless the rebellion comes first, and the man of lawlessness is revealed, the son of destruction. (2 Thess 2:1–3)

The Thessalonians were confused earlier about what happens to deceased believers, and now it appears they have had numerous people tell them that they have already missed the second coming of Christ and the Rapture. Notice that this is what Paul is writing about—Christ's second coming and the Rapture: "Now concerning the coming of our Lord Jesus Christ and our being gathered together to him . . ." When does the Rapture take place? This early church has been told they missed it, but Paul says they have not. In fact, Paul says, "For that day will not come, unless the rebellion comes first, and the man of lawlessness is revealed, the son of destruction" (2 Thess 2:3). What is "that day" that the Thessalonians have not yet missed? The day of "the coming of our Lord Jesus Christ and our being gathered together to him" (2 Thess 2:3). Paul says the day of the Rapture cannot come until "the man of lawlessness is revealed" (2 Thess 2:3).

Can we be certain the "man of lawlessness" Paul writes about in this passage is the same person who causes the abomination of desolation from Matt 24:15? The end of Dan 9:27 says, "And on the wing of abominations shall come one who makes desolate, until the decreed end is poured out on the desolator." The end that God has decreed for this person is poured out on him. That is judgment language against this evil ruler, so it would make sense that in 2 Thessalonians, Paul would call him "the son of destruction," either because he causes great destruction or because God has decreed destruction for him. It seems to become clearer that the person Paul is writing of is the same as the person behind the abomination of desolation Jesus mentions in Matt 24, which would be the same evil person as found in Dan 9.

> And the man of lawlessness is revealed, the son of destruction, who opposes and exalts himself against every so-called god or object of worship, so that he takes his seat in the temple of God, proclaiming himself to be God. (2 Thess 2:3b–4)

> So when you see the abomination of desolation spoken of by the prophet Daniel, standing in the holy place (let the reader understand) . . . (Matt 24:15)

This evil man will stand in the holy place inside the temple of God and proclaim himself to be God. Jesus says this is the abomination of desolation that will initiate the great tribulation. In Matt 24, Jesus says that the Rapture of the church will take place "immediately after the tribulation of those days" (Matt 24:29), but "for the sake of the elect those days will be cut short" (Matt 24:22). In 2 Thess 2, Paul says that Jesus will not come for the Rapture of the church until after this evil person is revealed, completely agreeing with the plain interpretation of Matt 24.

However, Paul does say something somewhat confusing in the next few verses:

> Do you not remember that when I was still with you I told you these things? And you know what is restraining him now so that he may be revealed in his time. For the mystery of lawlessness is already at work. Only he who now restrains it will do so until he is out of the way. And then the lawless one will be revealed, whom the Lord Jesus will kill with the breath of his mouth and bring to nothing by the appearance of his coming. (2 Thess 2:5–8)

Some interpretation needs to be done with this passage because several things are unclear, at least to the modern reader. In verse 6, Paul says, "And you know what is restraining him now." Paul is clearly writing about a topic he has shared with the Thessalonians before. Unfortunately, the modern reader isn't privy to all of the details that Paul shared with them on previous occasions. While the Thessalonians are likely fully aware of what Paul is referencing, we are left wondering who, exactly, is restraining whom from what.

Some will argue that this passage means that the Holy Spirit is restraining the antichrist until the appropriate time, and that the Holy Spirit will be "out of the way" after the Rapture takes place and the church is no longer in the earthly picture. Others will possibly say that the church is restraining the antichrist, and likewise will be "out of the way" after the Rapture.

I would like to confess to you that I do not know exactly "what is restraining him" in 2 Thess 2:6. It seems clear that the "lawless one" is restrained from being revealed until that restrainer is "out of the way," but who is that restrainer? The proponents of a pre-tribulation Rapture argue that the restrainer is the Holy Spirit or the church, believing that both of these will be "out of the way" when the Rapture takes place. There are two problems with this interpretation. First, the Holy Spirit is not mentioned anywhere in this passage to lead us to assume he is the restrainer Paul references. Second, this interpretation completely ignores the words of Paul from verses 1–4.

The pre-tribulation Rapture position argues that the order of end-time events begins with the Rapture, believing 2 Thess 2:5–8 shows that the church will be gone before the "man of lawlessness" is revealed. But 2 Thess 2:1–4 already informed the Thessalonians that "concerning the coming of our Lord Jesus Christ and our being gathered together to him . . . that day will not come, unless the rebellion comes first, and the man of lawlessness is revealed." Assuming that the man of lawlessness is the antichrist, Paul has expressly stated that the antichrist must be revealed *before* the Rapture. How, then, can one interpret verses 5–8 to say that the antichrist cannot be revealed until *after* the Rapture? This interpretation is incompatible with the verses that came immediately before.

Having already acknowledged that I don't have a definitive interpretation of "he who now restrains" in verses 5–8, I don't want to devote time to speculating who it *might* mean. The purpose of this study is to take what we do know and come to a reasonable conclusion regarding the Rapture, and this has already been accomplished in verses 1–4. This is strengthened by what Paul writes next:

> The coming of the lawless one is by the activity of Satan with all power and false signs and wonders, and with all wicked deception for those who are perishing, because they refused to love the truth and so be saved. Therefore God sends them a strong delusion, so that they may believe what is false, in order that all may be condemned who did not believe the truth but had pleasure in unrighteousness. (2 Thess 2:9–12)

In Matt 24:24–25, Jesus says, "For false christs and false prophets will arise and perform great signs and wonders, so as to lead astray, if possible, even the elect. See, I have told you beforehand." The antichrist and people associated with him will perform such convincing miracles that all unbelievers will be completely fooled. Even believers might have been convinced by these miracles had they not been thoroughly warned about them in advance by Jesus and Paul in Matt 24 and 2 Thess 2.

While Paul does not expressly mention the great tribulation, the deceptions he references in 2 Thess 2:9–10 are associated with the revealing of antichrist, which coincides with the deceptions Jesus mentions as happening during the great tribulation.

CONCLUSION

Twice in his first letter, 1 Thess 1:10 and 5:9, Paul writes that Christians will not experience God's wrath. However, the order he gives for our key terms is first the abomination of desolation, then the Rapture and the day of the LORD—which agrees with Jesus' order in Matt 24. If we assume that Paul's descriptions of the deception in 2 Thess 2:9–10 coincide with the great tribulation, then they actually match perfectly: abomination, tribulation, Rapture/day of the LORD.

Both Matthew and the letters to the Thessalonians describe the Rapture with very similar details: Jesus coming down from heaven, angelic involvement, a trumpet call, and believers gathered to him on the clouds. Both texts say that the Rapture will happen only after the antichrist is revealed. Both texts reveal that the day of the LORD will come like a thief, but only for unbelievers, because believers will know the order of events. The Christian will know that when the antichrist declares himself to be God in the third temple in Jerusalem, this marks the beginning of the great tribulation, and the great tribulation means that Jesus is coming soon. When he does, he will bring both the Rapture of the church and the judgment of the day of the LORD.

If Christians must experience the great tribulation, how can Paul write that they will not experience the wrath of God? The simplest explanation would be that the great tribulation is not the wrath of God. It is the worst event the world has ever seen and is at least underway before the Rapture happens, which would be followed by the day of the LORD, which *does* involve the wrath of God.

The final focus of this study will be the book of Revelation. Because of its size and complexity, it may be beneficial to first get a summary of the book before becoming involved therein to see if the details described there also agree with what Daniel, Matthew, and the letters to the Thessalonians have revealed.

5

Revelation Overview

PIECING TOGETHER WHAT SCRIPTURE has revealed, there is a future seven-year period for the nation of Israel where an evil ruler—the man of lawlessness, or antichrist—will make some kind of a contract or covenant with many people. During the first half of that time period, the people of Israel will have the third temple in Jerusalem and be allowed to offer up the sacrifices that the Old Testament prescribed. Halfway through that time, three and a half years in, this antichrist will stop the sacrifices, take his seat in the temple, and proclaim himself to be God. That is the abomination of desolation that Jesus says begins the great tribulation, which will also last for three and a half years. During that time, Jesus will come back riding on the clouds, Rapture the church, and usher in the day of the LORD.

That appears to be the consistent testimony of the writings in the New Testament. Is the book of Revelation in agreement about the order of these events? What does the last book in Scripture reveal about how all of these things will play out when the time finally comes?

Something we need to acknowledge before searching through this particular book is that we have moved into a very different type of literature. This isn't the same type of instructional letter as what Paul was writing to the Thessalonians. While it is prophetic in nature, like Matt 24 and Dan 9 and 11, it incorporates more imagery akin to other prophecies in the book of Daniel. Everything studied so far has been literal. Much of this last book is figurative.

As in the previous chapters, the focus will not be on every detail of this book, but rather on those things that seem to directly relate to the key terms: abomination of desolation, great tribulation, Rapture, and the day of the LORD. To avoid confusion, let's see how the whole letter flows from beginning to end.

In chapter 1, John, most likely the apostle, is stuck on the island of Patmos when Jesus Christ gives him a revelation, which comes as a string of visions. Chapters 2 and 3 are direct instructions from Jesus to seven churches in Asia Minor: the churches in Ephesus, Smyrna, Pergamum, Thyatira, Sardis, Philadelphia, and Laodicea. As chapter 4 begins, John is brought up into the heavenly throne room, getting a heavenly perspective of the events that are to come at the end times.

Chapter 4 describes the throne-room scene, God on the throne, four living beasts, and twenty-four elders. Chapter 5 has God sitting on his throne, holding a scroll with seven seals that no one can open except Christ, who appears in the vision as a "Lamb, looking as if it had been slain" (Rev 5:6 NIV). In chapter 6, Jesus opens six of the seven seals. As he opens each of the first four seals, a different horseman is sent into the world, each riding a different colored horse. These four horsemen seem to represent conquest, war, famine, and plague. At the fifth seal, the souls of believers killed during that time ask God to judge the world and avenge their deaths. The sixth seal has cosmic events similar to those seen in the passages about the day of the LORD.

There is a pause before Jesus opens the seventh seal, which he does at the beginning of chapter 8. Between the opening of the sixth and seventh seals, chapter 7 describes 144,000 faithful Israelites being given some kind of seal of protection before four angels are permitted to bring harm to the earth. John then sees a multitude of saints from all over the earth wearing white robes and standing in the heavenly throne room described back in chapter 4. Paul is told by one of the twenty-four elders that "these are the ones coming out of the great tribulation" (Rev 7:14).

Chapter 8 has Jesus opening the seventh seal. It is followed by seven angels each being given a trumpet, and six of the seven trumpets are blown in chapters 8 and 9. Each trumpet corresponds to something terrible happening on the earth. The seventh trumpet is not blown until the end of chapter 11, when loud voices proclaim, "The kingdom of the world has become the kingdom of our Lord and of his Christ" (Rev 11:15).

Before that seventh trumpet at the end of chapter 11, John appears to experience a scene change in chapter 10. Up to this point, he had been seeing everything from the perspective of the heavenly throne room described in chapter 4. In chapter 10, an angel comes to earth, with one foot on land and one on the sea, holding a little scroll. John is told by a voice from heaven to take that little scroll and eat it, so John must be down on the earth and not in the heavenly throne room during this particular vision. In chapter 11, John is instructed to measure the earthly temple, and is told about two witnesses who will prophesy for 1,260 days, or three and a half years. A "beast that rises from the bottomless pit" will kill them (Rev 11:7), but they will rise three and a half days later and be called up to heaven. Then, at the end of chapter 11, the seventh trumpet is blown and Jesus is declared the king of the world forever!

But the book doesn't end with chapter 11. There are more visions for John to record, this time appearing to be seen from the perspective of earth rather than the perspective of heaven. This leads the reader to believe that the book of Revelation is not written in a strictly chronological order. There is an overview of events from heaven's perspective in chapters 4–11, and the chapters that follow provide details surrounding these events.

In chapter 12, John sees a sign in heaven of a woman giving birth to a son. There is a seven-headed, ten-horned dragon who seeks to consume the child (Rev 12:3–4), but the child is snatched up to the heavenly throne room (Rev 12:5). The woman is sheltered in the wilderness for 1,260 days, or three and a half years (Rev 12:6). A great war breaks out in heaven between the dragon with his army of demonic angels and Michael the archangel, who leads the army of God's angels (Rev 12:7). The evil dragon is identified as Satan (Rev 12:9), and he is thrown to the earth, where more bad things start to take place.

Chapter 13 describes a beast coming out of the sea that is similar in description to the antichrist in other passages (Rev 13:1). There is another beast that comes out of the earth and makes the whole world worship that first beast (Rev 13:11–12). The 144,000 faithful Israelites from chapter 7 are seen again in chapter 14, standing beside the Lamb and singing a new song before the heavenly throne room (Rev 14:3). Three angels fly over the earth, the first proclaiming the gospel and coming judgment (Rev 14:6–7), the second declaring the fall of "Babylon the great" (Rev 14:8), and the third warning of the judgment that will come on anyone who follows the beast. Chapter 14 ends with two separate harvests—the first is harvested by someone "like a son of man" (Rev 14:14) and the second by an unnamed angel. The second harvest seems to be specifically for people to experience God's wrath, which begs the question: What is the purpose of the first harvest?

Chapter 15 introduces seven angels with seven final judgments that will complete the wrath of God (Rev 15:1). The angels are given seven bowls of wrath in chapter 16 in order to pour out those final judgments. Chapters 17 and 18 describe the punishment that befalls a woman called "Babylon the Great" (Rev 17:5; 18:2, 10, 21), and that leads to the very last part of the book.

Chapter 19 has loud worship in heaven that is fairly similar to the proclamation at the seventh trumpet in chapter 11. Chapter 19 continues with Jesus, "the Word of God" (Rev 19:13), riding in on a white horse (Rev 19:11), defeating the forces of evil, and throwing the two beasts from chapter 13 into the lake of fire (Rev 19:20).

In chapter 20, Jesus reigns on the earth for a thousand years, and then Satan, who had been bound for that time, is released and allowed to amass one final attack against Christ. Satan is defeated again and is now himself thrown into the lake of fire. God wins. The dead are judged at what is called the "great white throne" judgment (Rev 20:11).

Heaven and earth are destroyed and rebuilt perfectly in chapter 21, and the New Jerusalem comes down from heaven as the capital city of the perfected world. The book concludes with the promise that Jesus is coming soon. "Amen. Come, Lord Jesus. The grace of the Lord Jesus be with all. Amen" (Rev 22:21).

CONCLUSION

It seems clear that the key terms we have been studying are represented in this book. Numbers representing three and a half years are seen multiple times, matching up with the division of the final seven-year period described in Daniel. People will be worshiping the antichrist, an event Jesus and Paul said coincides with the abomination of desolation and the great tribulation. One of the seven seals from chapter 6 lines up with what Jesus describes when he talks about his second coming. There are two harvests in chapter 14, one of which sounds like it could be the Rapture. There are judgments that sound like they could be the judgments of the earth that come on the day of the LORD. All four key terms are represented in Revelation, helping with studying and determining the general timing of these events.

Jesus is described as a "Lamb who was slain" in chapter 5 (Rev 5:12), one "like a son of man" in chapter 14 (Rev 14:14), and as a rider on a white horse in chapter 19, which demonstrates some of Revelation's figurative language. Satan is described as a red dragon, while the antichrist is a beast coming out of the sea with ten horns and seven heads (Rev 13:1). These should best be understood as descriptions that reveal characteristics of these people without describing what they physically look like. Jesus doesn't literally have seven horns and seven eyes (Rev 5:6), but these descriptions probably represent the completeness of his power and knowledge.

With the overview complete, let's analyze "the revelation of Jesus Christ" (Rev 1:1) and what it reveals about the Rapture.

6

Revelation 1–4

IN REVELATION 1:19, JESUS tells John, "Write, therefore, what you have seen, what is now and what will take place later." Since the most frequently discussed future event in Scripture is the day of the LORD, one could assume that Jesus was revealing that this book will give insight into this eventual day, and possibly the other key concepts as well. However, no specific references to end-time events are seen in chapter 1.

In chapters 2 and 3, Jesus gives specific instructions to seven distinct churches: Ephesus, Smyrna, Pergamum, Thyatira, Sardis, Philadelphia, and Laodicea. Every church is given either encouragement, rebuke, or both. Ephesus was encouraged for its perseverance and for not "bear[ing] with those who are evil" (Rev 2:2), while they were simultaneously rebuked because they had "abandoned the love [they] had at first (Rev 2:4). Each message appears to be unique to that particular congregation, though every message ends with the phrases "He who has an ear, let him hear what the Spirit says to the churches" (Rev 2:7, 11, 17, 29; 3:6, 13, 22) and "The one who conquers . . ." followed by a promise related to eternal life (Rev 2:7, 11, 17, 26; 3:5, 12, 21).

The specific nature of each message would lead to the conclusion that each is unique to a particular church in Asia Minor. While every believer can apply the principles of each message, are the words in these two chapters directed at all believers at all times? The promises made to "the one who conquers" may apply to believers in general, but the specific encouragements and rebukes are certainly not directed to all believers. For instance, Jesus shares how two different churches have addressed "the works of the Nicolaitans" (Rev 2:6). One group hates these works (Rev 2:6), while the other has members who hold to those teachings (Rev 2:15). Jesus does not mention the Nicolaitans in his messages to the other five churches. These are specific issues for specific churches rather than universal statements.

DOES REVELATION 3:10 SUPPORT A PRE-TRIBULATION RAPTURE?

The promise that gets the most attention, at least relating to our study, is the one that is made to the church in Philadelphia in Rev 3:10 (NIV): "Since you have kept my command to endure patiently, I will also keep you from the hour of trial that is going to come upon the whole world to test those who live on the earth." The reason it gets the most attention is because proponents of the pre-tribulation Rapture hold this verse as a supporting text for the Rapture happening before the great tribulation. Is that necessarily what this promise is referencing?

The first thing to notice is that this is not part of the promise to "the one who conquers," which is found a little later, in verse 12. Revelation 3:10 reads more as a direct promise to those specific Christians because of what they had already done, rather than as a promise in response to what they will do in the future. "To him who overcomes" is a conditional promise based on future behavior, while the Christians in Philadelphia being free from this future test seems to be an unconditional promise in response to what they had already done. Would it, then, be a stretch to interpret this promise as applying to all believers and referencing a pre-tribulation Rapture?

Compare the words to Philadelphia to those given to Smyrna. Revelation 2:10 says, "Do not fear what you are about to suffer. Behold, the devil is about to throw some of you into prison, that you may be tested, and for ten days you will have tribulation. Be faithful unto death, and I will give you the crown of life."

Is this a universal promise to all believers for all time? Is Satan about to throw some of us into prison specifically for ten days? Or does it make more sense that Jesus is giving a specific warning to those Christians in Smyrna? If Rev 2:10 is specific to Smyrna, why would Rev 3:10 be universal instead of specific to Philadelphia?

Something else to consider is that what the Philadelphians are being kept from is not described as a tribulation, but rather as a trial, test, or temptation, depending on the Bible translation. The word Jesus used in Matt 24:21 and the word used in Rev 7:14, both translated as "tribulation," is not the same Greek word used in Rev 3:10.

Some interpreters believe that the seven churches are symbolic of seven "church ages," with Ephesus representing the early church and Laodicea representing the condition of the church just before the end-time events take place. One consideration regarding this interpretation is that the promise to be kept from "the hour of trial" (Rev 3:10) is not made to the final church, which would make this interpretation difficult to maintain. The promise is also not made to any of the other churches.

Because of the reasons listed above, it is unreasonable to believe that this verse necessitates a pre-tribulation Rapture. Now, I don't think many people are hanging their hats on this one verse, but it sounds more like hunting for a verse that could potentially support a position rather than truly studying the text and seeking to conform one's position to what is being revealed. This is especially true if the interpretive methods one uses for one text, like Rev 2:10, suddenly change in another, like Rev 3:10, when one prefers that verse to mean something that supports a particular view.

WHAT ABOUT THE ABSENCE OF THE WORD "CHURCH"?

Another popular pre-tribulation Rapture argument is that the words "church" and "churches," seen many times in the first three chapters, is not seen again until the final chapter of the book. Does

this interesting observation add some credibility to the pre-tribulation Rapture view?

First, we should ask whether the church might be mentioned
using any other words that could potentially describe it. If, for instance, Revelation contained the phrase "the body of Christ," even
though it isn't the word "church," from how that phrase has been
used elsewhere in the New Testament, one would interpret that
phrase as representative of the church. Even in Rev 19, though the
word "church" isn't used, there is the phrase "his bride has made
herself ready" (Rev 19:7). Does the "bride" represent the church?
The following verse seems to support that interpretation:

> "It was granted her to clothe herself with fine linen, bright
> and pure"—for the fine linen is the righteous deeds of the
> saints. (Rev 19:8)

If "the saints" are Christians, then the church is mentioned in
Rev 19, just not using that particular word. Instead, the church is
described as the bride of Christ, consisting of the saints, or Christians, who are beautifully adorned with their righteous acts. The
church has consistently been pictured as the bride of Christ in other
New Testament passages:

> For I feel a divine jealousy for you, since I betrothed you
> to one husband, to present you as a pure virgin to Christ.
> (2 Cor 11:2)

> So that he might present the church to himself in splen-
> dor, without spot or wrinkle or any such thing, that she
> might be holy and without blemish. In the same way
> husbands should love their wives as their own bodies. He
> who loves his wife loves himself. (Eph 5:27–28)

The word "church" has not been seen in chapters 4–21. But
"bride" and "saints" have been used. If the "bride" is the church and
the "saints" are the church in chapter 19, then any other usage of
the word "saints" at least *could* be representative of the church. Are
such occurrences found in Revelation? In fact, the word "saints"
appears in thirteen different verses in Revelation, all after chapter
3. The word is found in 5:8, 8:3, 8:4, 11:18, 13:7, 13:10, 14:12, 16:6,

17:6, 18:20, 18:24, 19:8, and 20:9. That is a large number of potential references to the church.

There are ways in which these verses can be explained to support a pre-tribulation Rapture view. If you presuppose that the church was raptured before the messy middle of Revelation, then maybe these saints are those who convert after the Rapture, or maybe they are the 144,000 faithful Israelites mentioned in chapters 7 and 14. The problem with either of these conclusions is the fact that they presuppose something that has not been expressly stated, or even clearly implied, in Scripture.

Like with Rev 3:10, the observation that the word "church" was not used in chapters 4–21 doesn't necessarily mean that the church itself is not present on earth during these events. That leaves one more verse that could potentially be used to support a pre-tribulation Rapture.

DOES REVELATION 4:1 SUPPORT A PRE-TRIBULATION RAPTURE?

In Rev 4, John is brought up into the heavenly throne room, where he sees God, four living beasts, and twenty-four elders. Verse 1 is where he is called from the island of Patmos to that heavenly place:

> After this I looked, and behold, a door standing open in heaven! And the first voice, which I had heard speaking to me like a trumpet, said, "Come up here, and I will show you what must take place after this." (Rev 4:1)

Is this some kind of a veiled reference to the fact that believers, like John, will be caught up to heaven before all of the events that John sees take place? This doesn't seem to be the interpretation of most scholars, even those who hold to a pre-tribulation Rapture. If John moving locations in his visions is symbolic of the church moving locations, then what do we do with Rev 10:8–9?

> Then the voice that I had heard from heaven spoke to me again, saying, "Go, take the scroll that is open in the hand of the angel who is standing on the sea and on the land."

So I went to the angel and told him to give me the little
scroll. And he said to me, "Take and eat it; it will make
your stomach bitter, but in your mouth it will be sweet as
honey." (Rev 10:8–9)

John appears to leave the heavenly throne room and go back
down to earth to grab a scroll from an angel who is standing on
earth with one foot on land and one on water. If Rev 4:1 moves the
church to heaven, by that same logic Rev 10:9 might move it back
down to earth. The alternative interpretation of Rev 4:1 is that John
is personally being called up in a vision to gain insight into what is
going to take place in future events, not serving as a symbol of the
church being raptured.

CONCLUSION

There does not seem to be any convincing evidence that any of the
passages in Rev 1–4 help to understand the timing of the Rapture.
The church might be referenced in the middle chapters as the
"saints," and the promise that the church in Philadelphia will not
go through "the hour of trial that is going to come upon the whole
world" (Rev 3:10) is not guaranteed to be a universal promise to all
believers that they will not go through the great tribulation. Certainly, John being called up in a vision is not the same as the church
being called up at the Rapture.

7

Revelation 5–6

IN REVELATION CHAPTER 4, John is called up to the heavenly throne room. In chapter 5, Jesus joins that scene as the only person qualified to take the scroll with seven seals from the right hand of the Father and open it. Chapter 6 is devoted to what happens as Jesus opens up six of those seven seals.

SEALS ONE THROUGH FOUR:
THE FOUR HORSEMEN

> Now I watched when the Lamb opened one of the seven seals, and I heard one of the four living creatures say with a voice like thunder, "Come!" And I looked, and behold, a white horse! And its rider had a bow, and a crown was given to him, and he came out conquering, and to conquer. (Rev 6:1–2)

The first four seals each have an associated rider on a horse of a certain color: a white horse for seal one, a red horse for seal two, a black horse for seal three, and a pale green horse for seal four. While people don't tend to try to identify an individual rider for each of the other seals, there is a tendency for people to do so with the first horseman. Most often, the rider associated with this first seal is the antichrist. Sometimes it is interpreted as Jesus, but that doesn't fit well with everything else revealed in the book. Jesus is riding a white horse in Rev 19, but he is clearly identified as "the Word of God" (Rev 19:13), which is the name that the author of Revelation gave Jesus at the beginning of his gospel in John 1:1. In Rev 19, he doesn't have a bow but instead a sword coming from his mouth. Also, Jesus is the Lamb opening the seals, so it would be strange to have Jesus represented by two different images in the exact same vision at the opening of the first seal.

Meanwhile, the antichrist would fit the context of what is being presented in chapter 6, though the rider on the white horse may not be intended to personify him. The whole world will follow him, and him setting himself up as God in the temple will initiate the great tribulation, which may be represented by the next three seals.

When Jesus breaks open the second seal, a rider comes out on a red horse and takes peace away from the earth. Trying to relate this to what Jesus describes in Matt 24, this may be part of the great tribulation. The third seal brings a rider on a black horse that ushers in famine, where a full day's wages will only be enough to buy food for a single person to survive for a single day. Finally, the fourth seal brings in the personification of death riding a pale horse.

> And I looked, and behold, a pale horse! And its rider's name was Death, and Hades followed him. And they were given authority over a fourth of the earth, to kill with sword and with famine and with pestilence and by wild beasts of the earth. (Rev 6:8)

Sword, famine, and disease seem to be the outcomes of the second, third, and fourth seals being opened. If the first rider does represent the antichrist, it would make sense that these next three seals represent the great tribulation. Twenty-five percent of the world's population will be destroyed in a time window of only three and a half years. The words of Jesus ring true when he says, "There will be great tribulation, such as has not been from the beginning of the world until now" (Matt 24:21).

Another possibility is that the first four seals represent the first three and a half years of the final seven-year period, as opposed to the great tribulation that will take place during the second three and a half years. However, it would be difficult to imagine that a quarter of the population dying in that short of a time could be caused by anything other than the great tribulation.

SEAL FIVE: WHERE IS GOD'S WRATH?

There is a difference between this fifth seal and the four that came before it. When this seal is removed from the scroll, no rider comes out. No great catastrophe is described. That calls for careful consideration of the meaning of this fifth seal.

> When he opened the fifth seal, I saw under the altar the souls of those who had been slain for the word of God and for the witness they had borne. They cried out with a loud voice, "O Sovereign Lord, holy and true, how long before you will judge and avenge our blood on those who dwell on the earth?" Then they were each given a white robe and told to rest a little longer, until the number of their fellow servants and their brothers should be complete, who were to be killed as they themselves had been. (Rev 6:9–11)

War, famine, and plague have killed a quarter of the world's population. At first glance, this seems like the wrath of God being poured out on the earth. This is a terrible time, the likes of which the world has never seen. However, two details catch the reader's attention.

First, the souls under the altar have been "slain for the word of God and for the witness they had borne" (Rev 6:9). These are Christians that were killed for their faith, and in context, it would make sense if they were killed during the great tribulation of the prior four seals. It says more Christians are going to be killed "until the number . . . should be complete" (Rev 6:11). It sounds like a lot of Christians are going to be killed in the great tribulation, which would sound strange if we were to assume that the Rapture will happen before that terrible time.

Who are these souls under the altar? If they are all the martyrs of Christianity over all of human history, that would go against the request they make for God to "judge and avenge our blood on those who dwell on the earth" (Rev 6:10). It seems that these souls were killed specifically during the first four seals—the great tribulation—and that they are asking God to avenge their deaths on the people still alive on the earth at that moment.

The second interesting detail in this passage is the question that these souls ask the Father: "how long before you will judge and avenge . . . ?" While war, famine, and plague have covered the earth, the souls under the altar do not view this as the judgment of God. Given 1 Thess 1:10 and 5:9, which promise that believers will not experience the wrath of God, are used to argue that Christians will not experience the great tribulation, the words of these souls require careful consideration. For these souls, the great tribulation has come, and yet they ask the Father when he will avenge them by judging the earth.

Perhaps the great tribulation is not the wrath of God. The key term associated with the wrath of God is the day of the LORD. It is described in Isa 34:8 as "a day of vengeance," and in Jer 46:19 as a day "to avenge himself on his foes." That sounds like what the souls are asking for, as if it didn't happen during the events of the first four seals. And from what is seen in the Old Testament, it doesn't sound like the day of the LORD has come yet in the book of Revelation.

> End-time order of operations:
> Cosmic signs → day of the LORD

The Old Testament book of Joel provides the following:

> The sun shall be turned to darkness, and the moon to blood, before the great and awesome day of the LORD comes. And it shall come to pass that everyone who calls on the name of the LORD shall be saved. For in Mount Zion and in Jerusalem there shall be those who escape, as the LORD has said, and among the survivors shall be those whom the LORD calls. (Joel 2:31–32)

The sun being turned to darkness and the moon having the appearance of blood are clear signs seen just *before* the day of the LORD. Those signs must come before that time of vengeance, and yet those signs have not been seen during the opening of the first five seals. However, those cosmic signs are present at the opening of the sixth seal.

SEAL SIX: COSMIC SIGNS

> When he opened the sixth seal, I looked, and behold, there was a great earthquake, and the sun became black as sackcloth, the full moon became like blood, and the stars of the sky fell to the earth as the fig tree sheds its winter fruit when shaken by a gale. (Rev 6:12–13)

At the opening of the sixth seal, the very signs mentioned in Joel 2:31–32 are now visible. The sun is being darkened and the moon looks like blood. The stars falling and the mentioning of a fig tree also draw attention back to the words of Jesus in Matt 24.

> Immediately after the tribulation of those days the sun will be darkened, and the moon will not give its light, and the stars will fall from heaven, and the powers of the heavens will be shaken. (Matt 24:29)

> From the fig tree learn its lesson: as soon as its branch becomes tender and puts out its leaves, you know that summer is near. So also, when you see all these things, you know that he is near, at the very gates. (Matt 24:32–33)

It is undeniable that what Jesus describes in Matt 24 is being seen now at the sixth seal in Rev 6. A side-by-side comparison reveals further parallels:

> The sky vanished like a scroll that is being rolled up, and every mountain and island was removed from its place. Then the kings of the earth and the great ones and the generals and the rich and the powerful, and everyone, slave and free, hid themselves in the caves and among the rocks of the mountains, calling to the mountains and rocks, "Fall on us and hide us from the face of him who is seated on the throne, and from the wrath of the Lamb,

for the great day of their wrath has come, and who can
stand?" (Rev 6:14–17)

Then will appear in heaven the sign of the Son of Man,
and then all the tribes of the earth will mourn, and they
will see the Son of Man coming on the clouds of heaven
with power and great glory. (Matt 24:30)

In Revelation, the people are trying to hide because they see
"the face of him who is seated on the throne" and "the Lamb." In
Matthew, they "see the Son of Man coming on the clouds." The
world is terrified at the appearing of Jesus in the heavens, and in
Revelation, it is made clear that "the great day of their wrath has
come." This further supports what was learned from the words of
the souls at the fifth seal: that the great tribulation seen in the first
four seals was not the wrath of God. When the sixth seal is opened,
the people of the earth recognize that the wrath of God has finally
come. It didn't come at the start of the great tribulation. It came
after the great tribulation was already underway.

This is consistent with everything seen in both the Old and
New Testaments. The day of the LORD brings the wrath of God. The
great tribulation is not the wrath of God. Even if Christians do go
through the great tribulation, this does not mean that they are experiencing the wrath of God, because those are two different events.

What else is supposed to happen when Jesus comes riding in
on the clouds of heaven?

And he will send out his angels with a loud trumpet call,
and they will gather his elect from the four winds, from
one end of heaven to the other. (Matt 24:31)

It might be helpful to again provide the parallel verse from
Mark.

And he will send his angels and gather his elect from the
four winds, from the ends of the earth to the ends of the
heavens. (Mark 13:27)

After the cosmic signs, Jesus comes, bringing with him the
day of the LORD, which is his judgment and vengeance that the
souls at seal five had asked for. He also calls his angels to gather up

believers from all over the earth, as well as the heavens. Consider the language used in Matt 24:31 and compare it to the language of 1 Thess 4:16–17.

> For the Lord himself will descend from heaven with a cry of command, with the voice of an archangel, and with the sound of the trumpet of God. And the dead in Christ will rise first. Then we who are alive, who are left, will be caught up together with them in the clouds to meet the Lord in the air, and so we will always be with the Lord. (1 Thess 4:16–17)

Jesus descends from heaven in Matt 24 and 1 Thess chapter 4. There is a trumpet call. Angels are involved. Both living and deceased believers are gathered together. The language indicates that these two passages are describing the same event. The signs that precede Jesus descending from heaven are seen at the sixth seal in Rev 6, meaning all of these passages are connected.

CONCLUSION

The six seals seen in Rev 6 are directly related to Matt 24 and 1 Thess 4. The first four seals appear to depict the antichrist and the great tribulation, resulting in the death of a quarter of the world's population. The souls under the altar at the fifth seal reveal that the great tribulation is not the wrath of God, which comes on the day of the LORD. That day is preceded by the cosmic signs seen at the sixth seal, where Jesus is seen in the heavens and "the wrath of the Lamb" has finally come (Rev 6:16). In both Matt 24 and 1 Thess 4, Jesus being seen in the heavens also begins the Rapture. If the Rapture happens at the sixth seal, the expectation would be for a new multitude of believers to be in heaven at this point in Revelation that weren't there before.

8

Revelation 7–11

JESUS HAS OPENED SIX of the seven seals on the scroll that the Father was holding in the throne room. The first four seals describe the great tribulation, with the antichrist riding in, followed by war, famine, and plague. A quarter of the world population dies as a result. Yet, at the fifth seal, the souls under the altar ask God when his vengeance will come against their persecutors, and they are told to wait a little longer. At the sixth seal, the earth sees Jesus coming in the sky, accompanied by the cosmic signs that were prophesied to precede the day of the LORD.

Before the seventh seal is opened at the beginning of Rev 8, John sees two important things take place in chapter 7. The first is that four angels who have authority to harm the land and the sea hold back what is probably the coming judgments of God until 144,000 faithful Israelites are sealed with a mark of protection from the wrath of God that is about to commence. This is consistent with the revelation from the fifth seal: the great tribulation is not the wrath of God. The great tribulation is focused on people, while the wrath of God is going to focus on the whole earth, not just the human population:

> Then I saw another angel ascending from the rising of
> the sun, with the seal of the living God, and he called
> with a loud voice to the four angels who had been given
> power to harm earth and sea, saying, "Do not harm the

earth or the sea or the trees, until we have sealed the ser-
vants of our God on their foreheads." (Rev 7:2–3)

It appears that the wrath of God is what will be seen in chapters 8–9 with the seven trumpets. A third of the earth is burned,
a third of the oceans ruined, and a third of the rivers—and even
a third of the light—is destroyed. At the sixth trumpet, a third of
humanity is killed. Unlike the four seals, these six trumpets focus
not just on people, but on the earth in general. A third of everything
is destroyed. But those 144,000 Israelites will be protected from this
harm. In Rev 9, the fifth trumpet has demonic creatures come up to
torment the people of earth, and yet the 144,000 will not be harmed:

> They were told not to harm the grass of the earth or any
> green plant or any tree, but only those people who do not
> have the seal of God on their foreheads. (Rev 9:4)

God's wrath has come upon the earth, but these events only
happen after the sixth seal, which means that the great tribulation has already been underway before these Jewish believers are
given divine protection. They are protected from God's wrath but
not necessarily from the great tribulation, which began before this
scene in Rev 7.

After John sees the 144,000 Israelites receive their mark of
protection, he sees another vision:

> After this I looked, and behold, a great multitude that
> no one could number, from every nation, from all tribes
> and peoples and languages, standing before the throne
> and before the Lamb, clothed in white robes, with palm
> branches in their hands. (Rev 7:9)

In chapters 4–5, the heavenly throne room is described as
having the Father on the throne, four living beasts, and twenty-
four elders, plus innumerable angels. All of these are seen again in
Rev 7:11:

> And all the angels were standing around the throne and
> around the elders and the four living creatures, and they
> fell on their faces before the throne and worshiped God.

According to Rev 7:9, human beings are now in the throne room, wearing white robes and worshiping the Father and the Son. The souls seen at the fifth seal had been given white robes to wear. Now, instead of having "souls" under the altar, we have a multitude of people standing in the throne room. What has changed? If Jesus coming at the sixth seal brought the Rapture, this all makes sense. There are people up in heaven who were not there previously because they were just raptured out of the great tribulation at the sixth seal. This multitude is identified a few verses later:

> Then one of the elders addressed me, saying, "Who are these, clothed in white robes, and from where have they come?" I said to him, "Sir, you know." And he said to me, "These are the ones coming out of the great tribulation. They have washed their robes and made them white in the blood of the Lamb." (Rev 7:13–14)

Notice that these believers have come "out of the great tribulation." It doesn't say they came out *before* the great tribulation. The simplest interpretation of this phrase would indicate that they were previously in the great tribulation, but that now they are out of it. These believers were on earth while the antichrist ushered in war, famine, and plague, but now they have been taken out of the great tribulation when Jesus appears, riding on the clouds of heaven. Jesus takes all living believers out of the world before he brings his wrath upon it, just as was promised in 1 Thessalonians. Believers will not experience God's wrath, because they won't be on earth to experience it. They were on earth to experience the antichrist's great tribulation but not the day of the LORD, with the exception of the 144,000 sealed Israelites, who are still seen on earth in Rev 9:4 during the wrath of God.

Rev 8 has Jesus open the final seal:

> When the Lamb opened the seventh seal, there was silence in heaven for about half an hour. Then I saw the seven angels who stand before God, and seven trumpets were given to them. (Rev 8:1–2)

There is general consensus that these seven trumpets *do* represent the wrath of God and his judgment on the earth. This is, however, entirely distinct from the great tribulation, which is represented by the first four seals. Before the wrath of God happens, the Rapture happens. This is consistent with everything studied so far.

Just like with the seven seals, there is a break in the action between the sixth trumpet and the final one. In chapter 10, John goes down to earth to take a little scroll from an angel that has one foot on land and the other on the sea. In chapter 11, John is commanded to "Rise and measure the temple of God and the altar and those who worship there, but do not measure the court outside the temple; leave that out, for it is given over to the nations, and they will trample the holy city for forty-two months" (Rev 11:1-2).

Forty-two months is three and a half years, but which time period is being presented here? Is this the three and a half years where Israel is permitted to make their sacrifices to God in the third temple, or the following three and a half years of the great tribulation? What divides these two periods is the abomination of desolation, the moment when the antichrist declares himself as God in the temple. Getting a definitive answer on which part of the seven-year period is referenced in Rev 11:2 is not strictly necessary for this study. What *is* necessary is the following verse:

> And I will grant authority to my two witnesses, and they will prophesy for 1,260 days, clothed in sackcloth. (Rev 11:3)

While these two witnesses are not identified by name, it is reasonable to assume that one of them is the prophet Elijah. On the mount of transfiguration, Jesus was seen by Peter, James, and John, and was accompanied by two Old Testament saints: Moses and Elijah.

> And after six days Jesus took with him Peter and James and John, and led them up a high mountain by themselves. And he was transfigured before them, and his clothes became radiant, intensely white, as no one on earth could bleach them. And there appeared to them Elijah with Moses, and they were talking with Jesus. (Mark 9:2-4)

Elijah was also prophesied about in Mal 4 as a sign that was to precede the day of the LORD.

> Remember the law of my servant Moses, the statutes and rules that I commanded him at Horeb for all Israel. Behold, I will send you Elijah the prophet before the great and awesome day of the LORD comes. (Mal 4:4–5)

Verse 4 mentions Moses, and verse 5 says Elijah comes before the day of the LORD. Those two prophets both appear when Jesus is transfigured. In Rev 11, there are two witnesses who prophesy on earth for three and a half years. According to Rev 11:7, the "beast that comes up from the abyss" kills them, but then three and a half days later they rise from the dead and get called up into heaven.

This is the order of events described in Joel and Malachi:

End-time order of operations:
Cosmic signs ➔ day of the LORD
Elijah ➔ day of the LORD

In Rev 11, it appears that Elijah has come. Elijah's ascension to heaven in Rev 11:12 is associated with the second woe in verse 14. These woes are introduced in Rev 8:13 as being associated with the final three trumpet judgments. If Elijah's ascension after three and a half years of prophesying coincides with the sixth trumpet judgment, which takes place during the wrath of God, then Elijah must have been prophesying during the three-and-a-half-year great tribulation, as opposed to the three and a half years before it. This is important because it fulfills that prophetic detail from Mal 4:5. Elijah has come before Jesus. Jesus comes to rapture the church at the sixth seal, after the great tribulation is already underway, while Elijah has been preparing the way for Jesus all during that time.

Seeing these two witnesses has also done something significant to the chronological order of the book of Revelation. Previously, everything in the book seemed to move forward in a chronological fashion: great tribulation, cosmic signs, Jesus in the clouds, Rapture, and then the day of the LORD. The discussion of these two witnesses breaks that chronological flow. Since this has happened with this vision, it would make sense that other visions could do the same thing. Context will be important in the rest of Revelation to determine where each vision takes place in the order of end-time events.

After the chronological break of Rev 10 and most of chapter 11, Rev 11:15 brings the reader back to the final trumpet, where "the kingdom of the world has become the kingdom of our Lord and his Christ, and he shall reign forever and ever." It appears that the wrath of God has been completed and that Jesus is now ruling the world. Jesus reigns on earth for a thousand years in Rev 20, so it is possible that Rev 12–19 will go back over all of the end-time events again, filling in details, whereas chapters 6–11 served more as an overview.

CONCLUSION

This section of Revelation further supports the understanding that the order of end-time events is as follows: abomination of desolation, great tribulation, Rapture, day of the LORD. The sixth seal saw Jesus in the sky after the prophesied cosmic signs, and before the seventh seal was opened, a great multitude of believers appeared in the heavenly throne room that were not present before that time. They were identified as "the ones coming out of the great tribulation" (Rev 7:14). At the sixth seal, after the great tribulation is already underway, Jesus appears in the sky to rapture the church. Immediately after that, the seventh seal is opened and the wrath of God begins.

Nothing indicates that the three and a half years of the great tribulation is concluded before Jesus comes at the sixth seal. Matt 24:36 says, "concerning that day and hour no one knows." The day of the Rapture is a mystery. This would not be the case if it was exactly 1,260 days after the abomination of desolation. However, it would still be a mystery if it was supposed to happen somewhere in that 1,260-day window. The most biblically consistent view regarding the timing of the Rapture is that it occurs somewhere during the great tribulation, specifically at the sixth seal. Christians alive at that moment could reasonably be called Revelation's Seal Team Six.

9

Revelation 12–16

THE GREAT TRIBULATION IS described in the first four seals. At the sixth seal, the cosmic signs that are supposed to come before the day of the LORD appear. Then, seven trumpets sound that describe the wrath of God coming upon the world. At the seventh trumpet, "the kingdom of the world has become the kingdom of our Lord and of his Christ" (Rev 11:15). Looking at chapters 12–16, it looks like these same events are described again, just from a different perspective.

REVELATION 12

In chapter 12, John sees a vision of a red dragon trying to devour the male baby of a pregnant woman wearing a crown of twelve stars. In verse 9, that dragon is identified as Satan, and the woman is likely symbolic of the nation of Israel. The male child would represent Jesus, "who is to rule all the nations with a rod of iron" (Rev 12:5). Of course, Satan does not devour Jesus, but verse 6 says something very interesting about the woman:

> And the woman fled into the wilderness, where she has
> a place prepared by God, in which she is to be nourished
> for 1,260 days. (Rev 12:6)

Israel is protected from Satan for three and a half years, or 1,260 days. Looking at the timing shared in Dan 9 and Matt 24, there is a seven-year time for Israel where the first three and a half years see relative peace and the nation is allowed to make sacrifices in their third temple in Jerusalem. After those years of sacrifices, the abomination of desolation takes place in the temple, and the next three and a half years carry the great tribulation. When John first saw these things taking place in chapter 6, it was from the perspective of the heavenly throne room. Now he may be getting a down-to-earth view of these future events.

Chapter 12 continues with a great battle in heaven between Satan with his angels and the archangel Michael leading angels of his own. Michael wins, and Satan and his angels are cast out of heaven and onto the earth. The vision indicates that Satan tries to attack Israel but fails, so he turns his attention instead to another group:

> Then the dragon became furious with the woman and went off to make war on the rest of her offspring, on those who keep the commandments of God and hold to the testimony of Jesus. (Rev 12:17)

The simplest interpretation of this verse is that Satan is now on the earth and waging war against the Christians. If this takes place after the three and a half years of peace, then Satan begins waging war against Christians at the beginning of the great tribulation. If Satan is able to wage war against Christians, this would indicate that there are Christians on earth for him to wage war against. In chapters 6–7, there is no indication that the Rapture takes place until after the great tribulation has already begun. Now that the clock has reset and these events are described again, the same holds true this time as well. There is no indication in chapter 12 that the church has been raptured before the great tribulation.

REVELATION 13

This chapter in Revelation describes two beasts, one coming out of the sea and another coming out of the earth, but the focus in this study of the Rapture will be on the section concerning the first beast, Rev 13:1–10, because it appears that Christians are being mentioned in this passage. The first beast is described using language very similar to the language used in a vision from Dan 7. This beast appears to be the antichrist empowered by Satan, since "the dragon gave the beast his power and his throne and great authority" (Rev 13:2 NIV). True to his name, the antichrist mimics the miracle of the true Christ, looking as if he had died and risen from the dead. The entire unbelieving world will follow after this imposter. Compare the description of his activities with what is described in 2 Thess 2.

> And the beast was given a mouth uttering haughty and blasphemous words, and it was allowed to exercise authority for forty-two months. It opened its mouth to utter blasphemies against God, blaspheming his name and his dwelling, that is, those who dwell in heaven. (Rev 13:5–6)

> Let no one deceive you in any way. For that day will not come, unless the rebellion comes first, and the man of lawlessness is revealed, the son of destruction, who opposes and exalts himself against every so-called god or object of worship, so that he takes his seat in the temple of God, proclaiming himself to be God. (2 Thess 2:3–4)

Paul tells the Thessalonians that "the coming of our Lord Jesus Christ and our being gathered together to him" (2 Thess 2:1) will not take place until the "man of lawlessness," the antichrist, sets himself up as God in the temple (2 Thess 2:3). According to Rev 13, he will be allowed to exercise authority for three and a half years, or forty-two months. Most likely, the 1,260 days from Rev 12:6 and 12:14 when Israel is protected represent the first three and a half years, and now these forty-two months represent the other half, which is the great tribulation. If the church is raptured before the great tribulation, why does Paul say the antichrist must be revealed first? If the church is raptured before the great tribulation, how can the antichrist do what is described in verse 7?

> Also it was allowed to make war on the saints and to conquer them. And authority was given it over every tribe and people and language and nation. (Rev 13:7)

The purpose of the entire book of Revelation is given in chapter 1, where John is told to "write on a scroll what you see and send it to the seven churches . . . Write, therefore, what you have seen, what is now and what will take place later" (Rev 1:11, 19 NIV). This entire letter is for the edification and encouragement of the church. Now, the church is being given very specific details about what is going to happen during the great tribulation. Knowing that the antichrist is going to deceive the whole world and wage war against Christianity, Jesus gives the church this encouragement:

> If anyone has an ear, let him hear: If anyone is to be taken captive, to captivity he goes; if anyone is to be slain with the sword, with the sword must he be slain. Here is a call for the endurance and faith of the saints. (Rev 13:9–10)

Every generation of Christians has read the encouragement of Rev 13:10. The antichrist is going to wage war against Christianity and kill as many believers as he can during the great tribulation. This time period is not described as the wrath of God. This was seen at the fifth seal, when, after the first four seals described the great tribulation, the souls under the altar ask the following:

> They cried out with a loud voice, "O Sovereign Lord, holy and true, how long before you will judge and avenge our blood on those who dwell on the earth?" (Rev 6:10)

When Satan is kicked out of heaven and down to earth, the loud voice from heaven declares:

> Therefore, rejoice, O heavens and you who dwell in them! But woe to you, O earth and sea, for the devil has come down to you in great wrath, because he knows that his time is short! (Rev 12:12)

The great tribulation is not the wrath of God. It is the wrath of Satan. While Christians have been given the promise in 1 Thessalonians that they will not experience God's wrath, they have never received a promise that indicates that they will not experience the wrath of the devil. Throughout all of the passages related to the Rapture, not a single one has indicated that Christians are taken out of the earth before this terrible time. Instead, Jesus warns the church about what is coming, saying, "Here is a call for the endurance and faithfulness of the saints" (Rev 14:12).

REVELATION 14

Several different events are described in this chapter: Jesus stands with the 144,000 Jews from chapter 7 as they now sing a new song that only they are allowed to know. Then, three angels go out and make three declarations to the people of the earth. Finally, two separate harvests are described as the chapter draws to a close. While the actions of the 144,000 may not be directly related to this study, the words of the angels and the events surrounding the two harvests appear to be related to the Rapture.

Here is what the first angel says:

> And he said with a loud voice, "Fear God and give him glory, because the hour of his judgment has come, and worship him who made heaven and earth, the sea and the springs of water." (Rev 14:7)

After chapter 13 has described the great tribulation, the first angel says God's wrath is now underway, meaning it wasn't underway before. This is consistent with descriptions from the seals and trumpets: the great tribulation is followed by the day of the Lord. The great tribulation is not the wrath of God but instead comes before it.

The second angel talks about Babylon the great, which isn't the focus of this study, so let's consider the third angel:

> And another angel, a third, followed them, saying with a loud voice, "If anyone worships the beast and its image and receives a mark on his forehead or on his hand, he also will drink the wine of God's wrath, poured full strength into the cup of his anger, and he will be tormented with fire and sulfur in the presence of the holy angels and in the presence of the Lamb. And the smoke of their torment goes up forever and ever, and they have no rest, day or night, these worshipers of the beast and its image, and whoever receives the mark of its name." (Rev 14:9–11)

That is a pretty direct message: don't worship the beast or take its mark unless you want to experience the wrath of God and be thrown into hell. The question is: Who is that message for? The whole world is going to follow the beast. Who would be listening to this angel's message and refusing to take the mark?

> Here is a call for the endurance of the saints, those who keep the commandments of God and their faith in Jesus. (Rev 14:12)

Like Rev 13:10, this is a message for Christians and an encouragement for them to persevere through this great tribulation. There are a lot of calls for perseverance for Christians when, presumably, they are not supposed to experience the events being described here. In fact, the next verse gives a promise to believers going through the great tribulation:

> And I heard a voice from heaven saying, "Write this: Blessed are the dead who die in the Lord from now on." "Blessed indeed," says the Spirit, "that they may rest from their labors, for their deeds follow them!" (Rev 14:13)

Many people are going to die during the great tribulation. According to Rev 6, a quarter of the world population is going to die in the wars, famines, and plagues that make up this event. Christians that are alive at this time are told to endure and refuse to worship the beast or to take his mark, even if that refusal leads to their death. In fact, those that die during this time are called "blessed," and the Spirit himself says "they will rest from their labor, for their deeds will follow them" (Rev 14:13). There is even a special blessing for those who are martyred during the great tribulation, as will be seen in Rev 20.

The last passage in Rev 14 describes two different people bringing in two different harvests. Here is the first one:

> Then I looked, and behold, a white cloud, and seated on the cloud one like a son of man, with a golden crown on his head, and a sharp sickle in his hand. And another angel came out of the temple, calling with a loud voice to him who sat on the cloud, "Put in your sickle, and reap, for the hour to reap has come, for the harvest of the earth is fully ripe." So he who sat on the cloud swung his sickle across the earth, and the earth was reaped. (Rev 14:14–16)

The one "like a son of man" is Jesus. In Dan 7, where the antichrist is described in similar language to that seen in Rev 13, Daniel also says this:

> I saw in the night visions, and behold, with the clouds of heaven there came one like a son of man, and he came to the Ancient of Days and was presented before him. (Dan 7:13)

All throughout the Gospels, Jesus speaks of himself as "the son of man." In Matt 24:30, Jesus says, "Then will appear in heaven the sign of the Son of Man, and then all the tribes of the earth will mourn, and they will see the Son of Man coming on the clouds of heaven with power and great glory." When the same cosmic signs appear at the sixth seal as Jesus describes in Matt 24, the people of the earth "[hide] themselves in the caves and among the rocks of the mountains" recognizing that the wrath of Jesus has finally come (Rev 6:15).

At the first harvest in Rev 14, where is Jesus? Seated on the cloud, just like in Matt 24:29–31. Who, then, would he be harvesting? The passage in Revelation doesn't say. It just says that "the hour to reap has come" (Rev 14:15), and Jesus reaps the earth. This is the first harvest mentioned in the passage. Here is the other one:

> Then another angel came out of the temple in heaven, and he too had a sharp sickle. And another angel came out from the altar, the angel who has authority over the fire, and he called with a loud voice to the one who had the sharp sickle, "Put in your sickle and gather the clusters from the vine of the earth, for its grapes are ripe." So the angel swung his sickle across the earth and gathered the grape harvest of the earth and threw it into the great winepress of the wrath of God. (Rev 14:17–19)

The purpose of the second harvest is clear: the wrath of God. What, then, was the purpose of the first harvest that Jesus did while sitting on the cloud? In order to be better equipped to answer that question, briefly consider chapters 15–16.

REVELATION 15–16

Having just seen the two harvests at the end of the previous chapter, John is back in the heavenly throne room. There, he sees seven angels with the final seven plagues that will wrap up the wrath of God. Those will get poured out on the earth in chapter 16, but before that, there is this scene:

> And I saw what appeared to be a sea of glass mingled with fire—and also those who had conquered the beast and its image and the number of its name, standing beside the sea of glass with harps of God in their hands. (Rev 15:2)

The word in the ESV is "conquered," but in most other translations, the phrase is "those who were victorious." What does that mean? Did these people in heaven actually defeat the beast, or does this mean that they remained faithful to God and to the warning given by the third angel in the previous chapter to not take the beast's mark or worship it?

What follows are the seven bowls of God's wrath in Rev 16. With all this in mind, what has been the sequence of events in chapters 12–16?

- Chapter 12: Israel is protected for three and a half years. Satan gets thrown down to earth and starts to wage war against Christians.

- Chapter 13: The antichrist blasphemes God and persecutes Christians, who are called to persevere.

- Chapter 14: Jesus, on a cloud, harvests one group of people. The purpose of this harvest isn't stated, but it isn't for God's wrath, because that is the express purpose of the second harvest that has been done by another angel.

- Chapter 15: People who have been "victorious" over the beast are now in the heavenly throne room, while the last seven plagues are prepared for pouring out the wrath of God.

- Chapter 16: The seven bowls of the wrath of God are poured on the earth.

These chapters reveal the following sequence: Satan tries to attack the nation of Israel, but she is protected for three and a half years, which is the first half of the final seven-year period for Israel. After this time, Satan turns his attention to Christians and wages war against them. Satan gives power and authority to the antichrist, who will be "blaspheming his [God's] name and his dwelling" (Rev 13:6), which appears to be the abomination of desolation that takes place in the third temple. The antichrist will exercise that authority for forty-two months and "make war on the saints" (Rev 13:7). This is the great tribulation that fills the second half of the final seven-year period. Saints are told to have "endurance and faith" during this time. Finally, Jesus appears in the clouds to reap one group of people before the other group gets gathered together to experience God's wrath. The group Jesus gathers must, therefore, be the Christians, meaning this reaping represents the Rapture, which takes place in the midst of the great tribulation. These newly raptured saints are then seen in heaven, having "conquered the beast and its image" (Rev 15:2) just before the seven bowls of God's wrath are poured out upon the earth.

That order of events agrees with everything studied so far. The final seven-year period for Israel will see relative peace for the first three and a half years. Then the abomination of desolation will begin the great tribulation, also lasting three and a half years. Then, Jesus comes riding on the clouds of heaven to rapture believers. Afterward, the wrath of God occurs.

Revelation 6–11 has the exact same sequence of events: the first four seals represent the great tribulation. The fifth seal reveals that the great tribulation was not the wrath of God. The sixth seal brings the cosmic signs signaling the coming of Christ. Then, before the seventh seal brings in the seven trumpets of God's wrath, a great multitude of people in heaven are identified as "they who have come out of the great tribulation" (Rev 7:14).

CONCLUSION

Matthew 24, 1 Thess 4, 2 Thess 2, Rev 6–11, and now Rev 12–16 all share the same sequence of end-times events, with no verses or passages seeming to contradict that order. The order of events is as follows: abomination of desolation, great tribulation, Rapture, day of the LORD. Not that the great tribulation has concluded before the Rapture, but rather that the great tribulation must begin before the Rapture can take place.

10

Summary, Defense, and Closing Remarks

ONE MIGHT HAVE EXPECTED another chapter in this book covering the last six chapters of Revelation. Truthfully, not much in those chapters deal with the Rapture. This makes sense, considering that the Rapture has already been described in Rev 7–14.

Revelation 19 mentions the wedding supper of the Lamb, as well as Jesus riding on a white horse to defeat the antichrist and throw him into the lake of fire. None of that changes the repeated order of events regarding the Rapture. Chapter 20 has the thousand-year reign of Christ on the earth, where it seems that those who died during the great tribulation are permitted to reign with Christ during that time before the great-white-throne judgment and before the new heaven and new earth are created. These are all beautiful, but they do not pertain to the Rapture. It appears that this study has drawn to a close.

Having surveyed the New Testament and carefully studied the relevant passages, there does not seem to be any verse or passage that indicates that the Rapture will take place before the seven-year period for Israel or before the great tribulation that begins halfway through it. Instead, all of the available evidence points to the Rapture taking place somewhere in the midst of that great tribulation, with many believers dying at the hands of the antichrist, though some will be victorious and survive to see Jesus gather them up in the clouds. Because no one knows exactly when Jesus will do this, it is reasonable to believe that the Rapture also does not take place *after* the great tribulation but instead takes place at some point during that period.

This may not feel like encouraging news. However, it is consistent with the multiple warnings given to believers regarding persecution:

> Indeed, all who desire to live a godly life in Christ Jesus will be persecuted. (2 Tim 3:12)

> For when we were with you, we kept telling you beforehand that we were to suffer affliction, just as it has come to pass, and just as you know. (1 Thess 3:4)

> Remember the word that I said to you: "A servant is not greater than his master." If they persecuted me, they will also persecute you. If they kept my word, they will also keep yours. (John 15:20)

> I have said these things to you, that in me you may have peace. In the world you will have tribulation. But take heart; I have overcome the world. (John 16:33)

Believers living through the great tribulation should lean on these encouraging words of Jesus: "But take heart; I have overcome the world" (John 16:33). Jesus tells us that we are blessed when we undergo persecution because our reward will be great in heaven (Matt 5:11–12). According to Rev 20:4–5, the believers that are killed during the great tribulation may receive an exclusive blessing: reigning with Christ on earth for one thousand years. Any suffering believers will face will be nothing compared to the riches of the eternal life all believers will have with Christ when the new heaven and the new earth are established as recorded at the end of the book of Revelation.

SUMMARY

The consistent testimony of Scripture is this: Jesus promises that just as he rose to heaven, he is coming back from heaven to take living believers to his heavenly home (John 14:2–4). When he comes to gather up living believers, those that have already died will be included as well (1 Thess 4:17). Jesus' coming for the Rapture, according to Paul, will include him descending from heaven, a loud command, the voice of an archangel, and a trumpet call (1 Thess 4:16). With very similar language, Jesus says he will come on the clouds of heaven, send out his angels with a trumpet call, and gather the elect together (Matt 24:30–31). In that moment, believers will be given their eternal bodies (1 Cor 15:51–53). Jesus' coming for the Rapture, however, will not occur until the great tribulation is underway (Matt 24:29). Paul's encouragement to those who think they have missed the Rapture (2 Thess 2:1–2) is that this event will not take place until after the abomination of desolation (2 Thess 2:3–4), which initiates the great tribulation (Matt 24:15, 21). While the Rapture will take place after the great tribulation has begun, no one knows the exact time Jesus will appear (1 Thess 5:12; Matt 24:36, 43), but his coming will be marked by cosmic signs (Matt 24:29, Joel 2:31).

The prophetic visions of Revelation reveal the exact same order of events: after the great tribulation (the first four seals), the cosmic signs that precede Jesus' coming are seen at the sixth seal (Rev 6:12–13), and before the seventh seal is opened, the church is taken out of the great tribulation (Rev 7:14). At the seventh seal, after the Rapture, the wrath of God appears in the form of seven trumpet judgments. That same order is repeated in the chapters that follow: Satan empowers the antichrist to make war with Christians (Rev 12:17; 13:2; 13:7), then Jesus gathers the church (Rev 14:14–16) before another angel gathers up the unbelievers for God's wrath (Rev 14:17–19), as seen in the seven bowls in chapter 16. The order of all of the related passages is the same: abomination of desolation, great tribulation, Rapture, day of the LORD.

DEFENSE

The position proposed here is known as the pre-wrath Rapture view, as opposed to the pre-tribulation, mid-tribulation, or post-tribulation views. Because the Rapture appears to take place at the sixth seal, I personally like to consider myself part of Revelation's Seal Team Six! There are certain aspects of the other three positions that do not seem to be consistent with the passages studied in this book.

The mid-tribulation view has the church being raptured at the midpoint of the seven-year period. However, according to our study, that time marks the abomination of desolation that begins the great tribulation. Both Jesus and Paul indicate that the Rapture takes place during the great tribulation, after the abomination of desolation rather than concurrent with it.

The post-tribulation view has the church experiencing all of the great tribulation. This is more consistent with Matt 24:29, where Jesus says, "Immediately after the tribulation of those days . . . ," but would harmonize poorly with the statements about that time being cut short for the elect (Matt 24:22) or that the timing of the Rapture is a mystery (Matt 24:36).

The position I am most familiar with—though I no longer hold to it—is the pre-tribulation view, which has a number of explanations that are used to support its position that may be worth careful evaluation in light of what has been studied. Consider some of the arguments made in favor of the pre-tribulation Rapture:

1. The church is not mentioned in Rev 6–18.

The word "church" or "churches" appears many times in Rev 1–3, but the word is noticeably absent from the book until the summary statement of Rev 22:16: "I, Jesus, have sent my angel to testify to you about these things for the churches. I am the root and the descendant of David, the bright morning star." Does the absence of the word "church" in chapters 6–18 prove a pre-tribulation Rapture?

The church is mentioned in Rev 19, but not with the word "church." Instead, it is called "the bride." This would imply that the church can be referenced without the word "church" being used. The church consists of believers in the Lord Jesus Christ. Believers are consistently called "saints," and "saints" are mentioned many times in Rev 6–18. Therefore, the church is mentioned in those chapters as still being on the earth. The prayers of the "saints" are before the throne in Rev 5:8, 8:3, and 8:4. "Saints" are identified as believers in Rev 11:18 and identified with the "bride" in Rev 19:8. "Saints" are told to persevere in Rev 13:10 and 14:12. The antichrist wages war against the "saints" in 13:7, and God's judgment is on those who shed the blood of the "saints" in Rev 16:6, 17:6, 18:20, and 18:24. Finally, as Satan's final attempt before being thrown into the lake of fire, Satan leads an army that "[surrounds] the camp of the saints and the beloved city" (Rev 20:9).

There is consensus that the "saints" in Rev 19:8 represent the church, so it would be presumptive to say that all of the other references to the "saints" in chapters 6–18 are not the church. The observation that the word "church" is not used in those chapters is interesting, but it certainly does not prove a pre-tribulation Rapture.

2. Revelation 3:10 promises that the church will be removed before the great tribulation.

Revelation 3:10 promises the church in Philadelphia that they will be kept "from the hour of trial that is coming on the whole world." Is that promise necessarily referring to the great tribulation? Is that promise of being kept from it universal to all believers? I don't think we can definitively say yes to either of those questions, but especially not to the second one. If this encouragement is universal for all believers, then every encouragement and exhortation in Rev 2–3 should also be universal. Is every church experiencing tribulation and poverty (Rev 2:9)? Is every church about to spend ten days in prison (Rev 2:10)? Does every church both hate the works of the Nicolaitans (Rev 2:6) and have some who hold to those same teachings (Rev 2:15)? If those things are not universally applied to every church, why then is Rev 3:10 universally applied? This inconsistency seems to come from a presupposition that a pre-tribulation Rapture is true, despite the fact that it has not been explicitly stated as true in Scripture.

3. We will not experience God's wrath, so we won't experience the great tribulation.

This argument presupposes that the great tribulation and God's wrath are the same thing. However, scripturally, this is not the case. It is true that Christians have the promise that they will not experience the wrath of God (Rom 5:9; 1 Thess 1:10, 5:9), but Christians are also told that they will experience tribulations (Matt 24:9, John 15:20, John 16:33, 2 Tim 3:12) and are not told they will avoid the great tribulation. The great tribulation is described in the first four seals in Rev 6, while at the fifth seal the souls under the altar ask God "how long before [he] will judge and avenge" (Rev 6:10), indicating that the great tribulation is not the wrath of God. In fact, this seems to be the wrath of the devil in the passage immediately preceding the antichrist persecuting the saints in Rev 13 (Rev 12:12).

Conflating the great tribulation and the day of the LORD is completely incompatible with Scripture. What were the signs that were supposed to come before the day of the LORD in the Old Testament? Sun darkened, moon turned to blood, and stars falling from the sky (Joel 2:31). Joel 2:31 specifically says that these things happen "before the great and awesome day of the LORD comes." When do those signs appear, according to Jesus? "Immediately after the tribulation of those days the sun will be darkened, the moon will not give its light, and the stars will fall from heaven . . ." (Matt 24:29). The great tribulation comes before the cosmic signs, which come before the day of the LORD. Those two events are completely different.

4. The church is singing in heaven during the great tribulation.

This comes from Rev 5:8–10, so let's consider that passage for a moment.

> And when he had taken the scroll, the four living creatures and the twenty-four elders fell down before the Lamb, each holding a harp, and golden bowls full of incense, which are the prayers of the saints. And they sang

> a new song, saying, "Worthy are you to take the scroll and to open its seals, for you were slain, and by your blood you ransomed people for God from every tribe and language and people and nation, and you have made them a kingdom and priests to our God, and they shall reign on the earth." (Rev 5:8–10)

This is before the seals are opened, and the ones singing are the twenty-four elders. Do these elders represent the church? Possibly. Do these elders represent the raptured church? No. The raptured church is suddenly present in the throne room in Rev 7, after the sixth seal. The raptured church is not seen in the throne room in Rev 5.

If one interprets the twenty-four elders to represent the church, they would have to represent the believers who have died before the great tribulation. Since nearly two thousand years have already passed since Christ's first coming and we are still waiting for his second coming, there are plenty of believers that these twenty-four elders could represent while not representing the raptured church.

5. There is a clear distinction between the Rapture and Christ's second coming.

What are the clear distinctions between these two events, and what scriptures are used to define these differences?

First difference: At the Rapture, Jesus comes "for" his saints. At the Second Coming, Jesus comes "with" his saints:

> It was also about these that Enoch, the seventh from Adam, prophesied, saying, "Behold, the Lord comes with ten thousands of his holy ones, to execute judgment on all and to convict all the ungodly of all their deeds of ungodliness that they have committed in such an ungodly way, and of all the harsh things that ungodly sinners have spoken against him." (Jude 1:14–15)

> So that he may establish your hearts blameless in holiness before our God and Father, at the coming of our Lord Jesus with all his saints. (1 Thess 3:13)

Both texts say "his holy ones" or "his saints," but is that necessarily speaking of human believers? In Jude, they are coming to execute judgment, something the seven angels do with the trumpet and the bowl judgments. Could the "holy ones" that Jesus is bringing be his angels rather than the church? Likewise, in Thess 3:13, Paul wants "your" hearts to be blameless before Jesus comes "with all his saints," or holy ones. Would that, then, mean that the group Paul identifies as "you" is not among "his saints"?

Alternatively, "his holy ones" could be the saints that have died before Jesus' second coming. All I'm seeking to point out is that these verses don't necessitate that the Rapture and the second coming are separate events. In fact, 1 Thessalonians seems to say otherwise:

> For the Lord himself will descend from heaven with a cry of command, with the voice of an archangel, and with the sound of the trumpet of God. And the dead in Christ will rise first. Then we who are alive, who are left, will be caught up together with them in the clouds to meet the Lord in the air, and so we will always be with the Lord. Therefore encourage one another with these words. Now concerning the times and the seasons, brothers, you have no need to have anything written to you. For you yourselves are fully aware that the day of the Lord will come like a thief in the night. (1 Thess 4:16–5:2)

Notice everything Paul says in this passage: Jesus is coming on the clouds to rapture the church. The Rapture is directly connected, in this passage, to "the day of the LORD." To say that the Rapture and the day of the LORD are completely separate events with multiple years between them would contradict not only everything studied up to this point but also the very flow of 1 Thessalonians, which is used to support the supposed separation between these events.

The Rapture and the day of the LORD are not synonymous any more than the abomination of desolation is synonymous with the great tribulation. In fact, the two pairings are quite similar: just as the abomination initiates the great tribulation, it appears that the Rapture initiates the day of the LORD. For both pairs, the one immediately precedes the other. The Rapture and the day of the LORD are not separated by seven years. They may only be separated by mere moments. Once the church is raptured, the true wrath of God, distinct from the wrath of Satan, can begin.

Second difference: At the Rapture, Jesus comes in the clouds. At the second coming, Jesus comes to the earth:

> For the Lord himself will descend from heaven with a cry of command, with the voice of an archangel, and with the sound of the trumpet of God. And the dead in Christ will rise first. Then we who are alive, who are left, will be caught up together with them in the clouds to meet the Lord in the air, and so we will always be with the Lord. (1 Thess 4:16–17)

> On that day his feet shall stand on the Mount of Olives that lies before Jerusalem on the east, and the Mount of Olives shall be split in two from east to west by a very wide valley, so that one half of the Mount shall move northward, and the other half southward. (Zech 14:4)

Let's evaluate the idea that Jesus being in different places—clouds and earth—means the Rapture and the second coming are two events separated by seven years. Before Jesus comes to the earth, doesn't he have to come down from heaven? Wouldn't it make sense for Jesus to be in the clouds just before coming to stand on the earth? The day of the LORD includes multiple things: seven trumpet judgments and/or bowl judgments, the battle of Armageddon, the antichrist being thrown into the lake of fire, and one thousand years later, another gathering of opposition to God before Satan is also thrown into the lake of fire. The Rapture takes place just before the judgments start. So, Jesus is in the clouds when he gathers the church for them to go to heaven before the day of the LORD, and once that day begins, he "stands" on the ground. That all flows logically and does not necessitate some seven years between the Rapture and the day of the LORD.

6. The trumpets of 1 Thessalonians and 1 Corinthians are not the same as in Revelation.

This seems to be a response to statements made in favor of the post-tribulation view, which may state that the seventh trumpet judgment—i.e., "last trumpet"—is when the Rapture takes place. I would agree with the thought that the trumpets of 1 Thessalonians and 1 Corinthians are not necessarily the same as every trumpet sounded in the book of Revelation. It is true that not every trumpet call in Scripture is one and the same. Context would be key in determining whether separate mentions of trumpets in different books of the Bible denote the same event.

This is less a proof of a pre-tribulation Rapture and more a critique of a different position. It doesn't prove a pre-tribulation Rapture at all.

7. The great tribulation is for Israel, not for the church.

Even if the above statement were true, this would not necessitate that the church be removed via the Rapture before the great tribulation takes place. This idea comes from the following text:

> Alas! That day is so great there is none like it; it is a time of distress for Jacob; yet he shall be saved out of it. (Jer 30:7)

There will be a terrible time that is described as "a time of distress for Jacob." That fits well with the words of Jesus in Matt 24, where the abomination of desolation takes place in the third temple in Jerusalem to initiate the great tribulation. Does this mean that the great tribulation will only be experienced by the nation of Israel? In Rev 6, the first four seals result in the death of a quarter of the world population. The whole world is experiencing the great tribulation, not just Israel. Likewise, the "elect" are mentioned in Matt 24, a term indicative of the church, not the nation of Israel.

The great tribulation is a part of Daniel's seventieth seven, but that does not mean that Christians will not go through it, or at least part of it. Remember the multitude of saints in Rev 7:14. They are described as being "the ones who come out of the great tribulation."

It doesn't make sense to "come out" of something if they were not originally in that event.

8. The Rapture can happen at any time. It is imminent.

When the word "imminent" is used to support the pre-tribulation Rapture, it essentially means that the Rapture can happen at any time and that no predicted intervening events need to take place before it occurs. Multiple Scripture references are offered to support this idea, including, but not limited to, the following:

> Be patient, therefore, brothers, until the coming of the Lord. See how the farmer waits for the precious fruit of the earth, being patient about it, until it receives the early and the late rains. You also, be patient. Establish your hearts, for the coming of the Lord is at hand. Do not grumble against one another, brothers, so that you may not be judged; behold, the Judge is standing at the door. (Jas 5:7–9)

> The end of all things is at hand; therefore be self-controlled and sober-minded for the sake of your prayers. (1 Pet 4:7)

> And let us consider how to stir up one another to love and good works, not neglecting to meet together, as is the habit of some, but encouraging one another, and all the more as you see the Day drawing near. (Heb 10:24–25)

> Children, it is the last hour, and as you have heard that antichrist is coming, so now many antichrists have come. Therefore we know that it is the last hour. (1 John 2:18)

These are the verses used to support a pre-tribulation Rapture. They say believers should "be patient" because "the end of all things is at hand." These are true statements, but they don't clearly state that the Rapture will take place at any time without some intervening events. In fact, when Heb 10 uses the phrase "as you see the Day drawing near," what might the writer be referencing? What do they see that tells them the time is near? In 1 John, what they are seeing are "many antichrists," and they know that the "antichrist is coming." How, exactly, does that verse promote the imminence of the Rapture? It looks like the signs they were seeing were precursors to the antichrist. The antichrist is actually a sign that precedes the Rapture, which is the opposite of what the pre-tribulation position states. But it is exactly what a pre-wrath position would expect:

> Children, it is the last hour, and as you have heard that antichrist is coming, so now many antichrists have come. Therefore we know that it is the last hour. (1 John 2:18)

> So when you see the abomination of desolation spoken of by the prophet Daniel . . . then there will be great tribulation . . . . For false christs and false prophets will arise and perform great signs and wonders, so as to lead astray, if possible, even the elect. . . . Immediately after the tribulation of those days the sun will be darkened . . . . Then will appear in heaven the sign of the Son of Man, . . . and he will send out his angels . . . , and they will gather his elect." (Matt 24:15–31)

> Now concerning the coming of our Lord Jesus Christ and our being gathered together to him, we ask you, brothers . . . . Let no one deceive you in any way. For that day will not come, unless the rebellion comes first, and the man of lawlessness is revealed, the son of destruction. (2 Thess 2:1, 3)

The pre-tribulation view says there is no necessary sign or event before the Rapture takes place, and yet all of the above passages say there is: the sign of the antichrist and the abomination of desolation. Even some of the very verses used to support the pre-tribulation view actually support the opposite.

9. Et cetera.

I'm sure there are numerous other proposed reasons to believe in a pre-tribulation Rapture, but all of them—that I have seen—have a similar tendency to either conflate different terms (such as the great tribulation being synonymous with the day of the LORD), misrepresent what the text actually says, or draw comparisons to other places in Scripture where people were saved from something. One example is the following: "God saved Lot from the judgment of Sodom; therefore, we won't go through the great tribulation." Again, this conflates the great tribulation with the wrath of God. Just because Lot was spared from that terrible event does not mean that Christians will be spared from the great tribulation. The one thing simply does not logically lead to the other. Other examples like the above were not listed because the same reasoning used in evaluating the listed proofs would disprove those others as well.

In short, I tried to compile a list of what appeared, in my estimation, to be the best reasons provided by the most reputable proponents of the pre-tribulation view. In each case, they failed either to prove a pre-tribulation Rapture or to disprove a pre-wrath Rapture. The pre-wrath, or Seal Team Six, position appears to be the most biblically consistent view on the timing of the Rapture when all of the evidence is carefully evaluated.

CLOSING REMARKS

In the end, this is an in-house discussion among believers regarding a future event that has been prophesied in Scripture. Unlike those prophecies that have already been fulfilled, we do not have the benefit of hindsight to verify whether our interpretation of prophecies regarding the Rapture is correct. This is not a salvation issue, and if we do not agree on the timing of the Rapture, that does not mean we cannot extend the right hand of fellowship to each other. We are all saved by grace through faith in Christ, whether we believe the Rapture will happen pre-tribulation, post-tribulation, or somewhere in between.

What I have tried to provide is a careful study of the relevant passages, making every effort to set preconceptions and presuppositions aside in order to, hopefully, determine the true order of end-time events. Can I say with 100-percent certainty that the view I hold is correct? Absolutely not. What I can say is that I came to this conclusion without presupposing any particular view beforehand. If I were prone to presuppose any view, then based on my upbringing in a Southern Baptist church, it would have been the pre-tribulation view. Hopefully, the above pages have proven—if nothing else—my intellectual honesty with regard to this discussion.

Your position in heaven is not determined by your views on the Rapture. Nor is your fellowship with other believers determined by it. No churches should break apart because of their differing opinions on the Rapture. While I consider this an important discussion, I do not find it worthy of breaking friendships, partnerships, fellowships, or anything else.

So, whether you agree with me or not, I would like to leave you with the following blessing from Num 6:24–26:

"The LORD bless you and keep you; the LORD make his face to shine upon you and be gracious to you; the LORD lift up his countenance upon you and give you peace." Amen.

The end.

Made in the USA
Las Vegas, NV
03 March 2022

44944145R00056